CA Colour Atlas of Medicine

Perry Choi, Atlas Editor
Blair Leonard and Jonathan Yeung, Editors-in-Chief

Third Edition

Copyright © 2005
Toronto Notes Medical Publishing 2005 Inc.

Cover Consultants: Blair Leonard and Jonathan Yeung

Notice

Canadian Cataloguing in Publication Data

The National Library of Canada has catalogued this publication as follows:

Main entry under title:

The Toronto Notes 2005: Review for the MCCQE
Annual.
Imprint varies.
ISBN 0-9685928-5-6 (21st ed.)

1. Medicine. I. University of Toronto. Faculty of Medicine.

R735.A1M33   610   C99-091498-6

Anesthesia

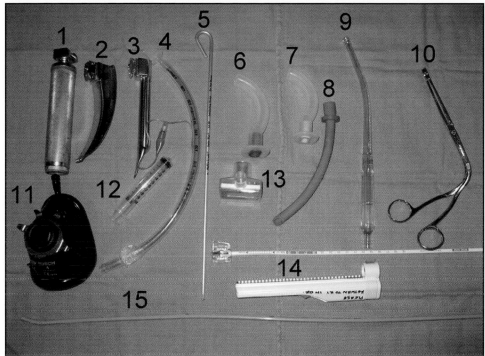

A1. Intubation Equipment
1. Laryngoscope handle
2. Macintosh III laryngoscope blade
3. Miller laryngoscope blade
4. Cuffed endotracheal tube
5. Stylet
6. Large oral airway
7. Small oral airway
8. Nasal airway
9. Yanker suction tip
10. McGill forceps
11. Face mask
12. Syringe
13. Carbon dioxide detector
14. Tracheal light
15. Bougie

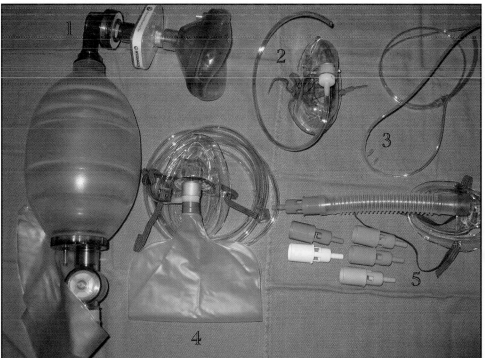

A2. Oxygen Masks
1. Ambu-bag (Laerdal resuscitator)
2. Simple face mask
3. Nasal prongs
4. Non-rebreather mask
5. Venturi mask with oxygen ports

Cardiac and Vascular Surgery

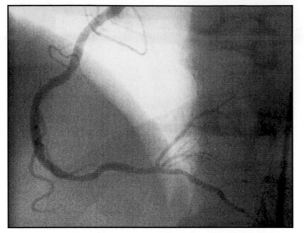

C1. Normal right coronary artery (RCA) with posterior interventricular (PIV) artery running inferiorly, and the posterior lateral branches branching superiorly in this view.
(Courtesy Toronto General Hospital Catheterization Laboratory)

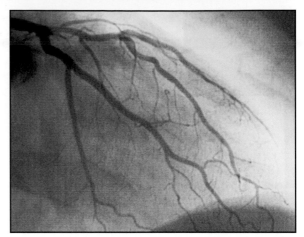

C2. Normal left coronary artery (LCA) with the circumflex system inferior to the left anterior descending (LAD) artery in this view.
(Courtesy Toronto General Hospital Catheterization Laboratory)

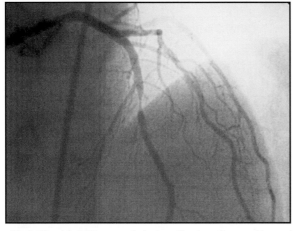

C3. LAD with 95% stenotic lesion distal to diagonal branches.
(Courtesy Toronto General Hospital Catheterization Laboratory)

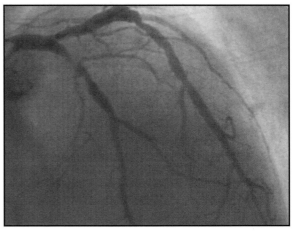

C4. Stenosis of the LAD, as well as the Circumflex.

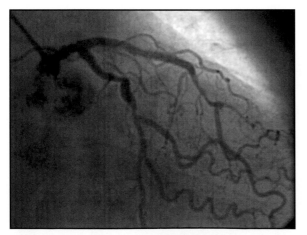

C5. This patient had two stents installed in this LAD, which you can see as cylindrical shapes within the vessel.

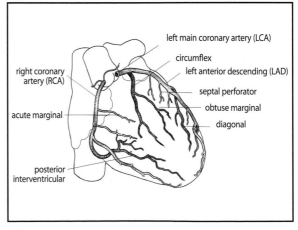

C6.

left main coronary artery (LCA)
circumflex
right coronary artery (RCA)
left anterior descending (LAD)
septal perforator
acute marginal
obtuse marginal
diagonal
posterior interventricular

Dermatology

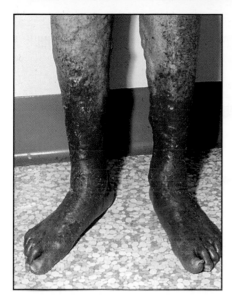

D1. Stasis Dermatitis
Erythematous scaling patches on lower legs. May see hyperpigmentation, swelling, and ulceration.
(Courtesy Dr. L. From)

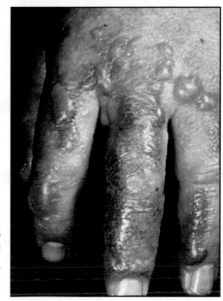

D2. Contact Dermatitis
Sharply demarcated, weeping and crusting papules and vesicles.

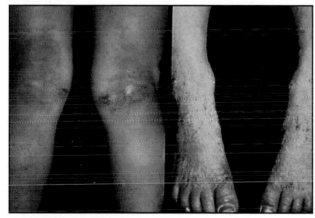

D3. Atopic Dermatitis
Excoriated, lichenified plaques with erythema, dryness, and crusting.

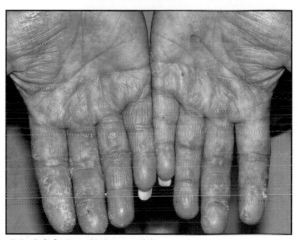

D4. Adult Atopic Dermatitis
(Courtesy Dr. S. Walsh)

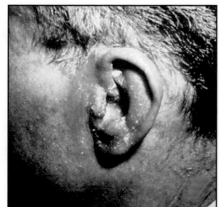

D5. Seborrheic Dermatitis
Diffuse within scalp margin, greasy yellow-white scales and underlying erythema.

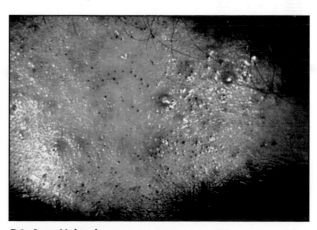

D6. Acne Vulgaris
Inflammatory papules, pustules, and open comedones.

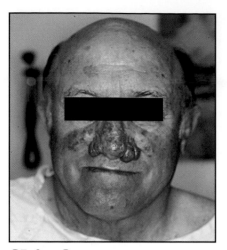

D7. Acne Rosacea
Prominent facial erythema, telangiectasia,
rhinophyma, and scattered papules.
(Courtesy Dr. L. From)

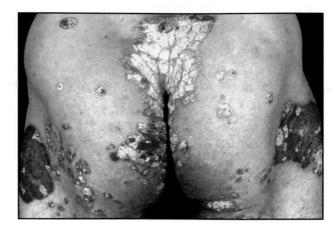

D8. Psoriasis
Dry, well-circumscribed, silvery scaling papules and plaques.
(Courtesy Dr. L. From)

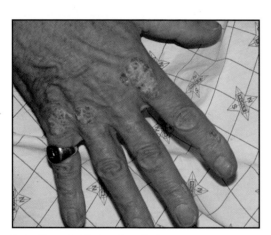

D9. Chronic Plaque Psoriasis
Dry, well-circumscribed, silvery scaling papules
and plaques. *(Courtesy Dr. S. Walsh)*

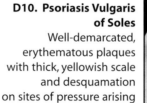

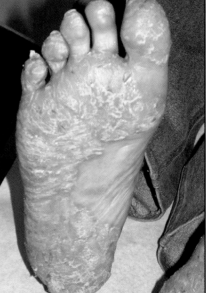

**D10. Psoriasis Vulgaris
of Soles**
Well-demarcated,
erythematous plaques
with thick, yellowish scale
and desquamation
on sites of pressure arising
on the plantar feet.
(Courtesy Dr. S. Walsh)

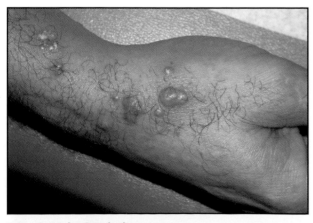

D11. Pustular Psoriasis
Deep-seated, dusky-red macules and creamy-yellow pustules
progress to hyperkeratotoic/crusted papules. Lesions are
confined to the palms and /or soles.
(Courtesy Dr. S. Walsh)

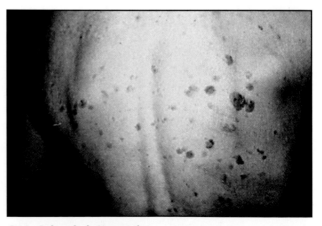

D12. Seborrheic Keratosis
Well-demarcated, waxy, brownish-black or tan
papules/plaques; warty and "stuck-on" appearance.

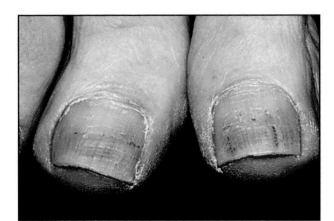

D13. Onychomycosis
Distal onycholysis, nail pitting, and subungual hyperkeratosis.

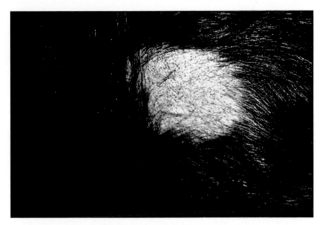

D14. Tinea Capitis
Diffuse area of mild scaling and hair loss with follicles present and occasionally erythema and pyoderma.

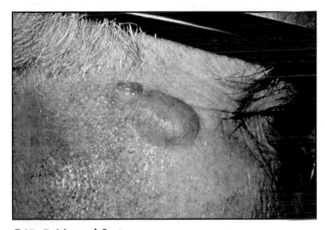

D15. Epidermal Cyst
Round, firm, yellow/flesh coloured, mobile nodule; may observe a follicular punctum on the overlying epidermal surface.

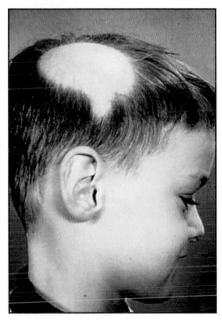

D16. Alopecia Areata
Sharply demarcated circular patch of scalp completely devoid of hair.

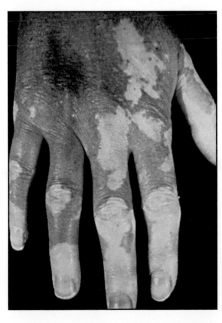

D17. Vitiligo
Typical acral distribution showing cutaneous depigmentation due to an acquired loss of melanocytes.

D18. Toxic Epidermal Necrolysis (TEN)
Widespread necrosis with painful blistering and denuding of epidermis.

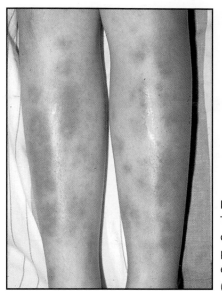

D19. Erythema Nodosum
Tender, poorly demarcated, deep-seated nodules and plaques usually on lower extremities.
(Courtesy Dr. M. Mian)

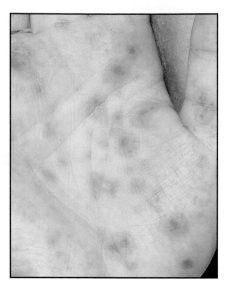

D20. Erythema Multiforme (EM)
Macules/papules with central concentric rings.
(Courtesy of Women's College Hospital Slide Library, Toronto)

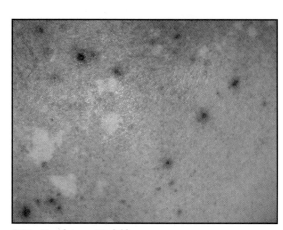

D21. Erythema Multiforme
(Courtesy Dr. S. Walsh)

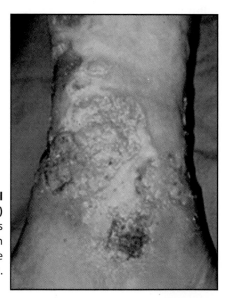

D22. Squamous Cell Carcinoma (SCC)
Indurated erythematous nodule or plaque with hyperkeratotic surface scale/crust and ulceration.

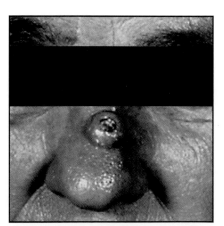

D23. Keratoacanthoma
Benign squamous exophytic nodule with central keratin-filled crater.

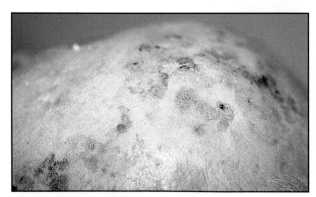

D24. Actinic Keratosis
Hyperkeratotic, erythematous, slightly elevated, flat-surfaced papules and patches on sun-exposed skin.
(Courtesy Dr. C. Forrest)

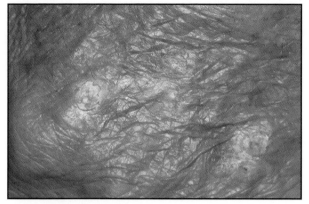

D25. Actinic Keratosis
(Courtesy Dr. S. Walsh)

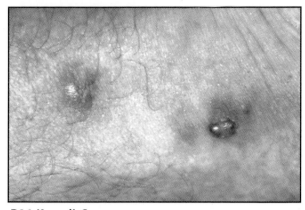

D26. Kaposi's Sarcoma
Bluish-red cutaneous nodules on the lower extremity.
(Courtesy Dr. J. Murray)

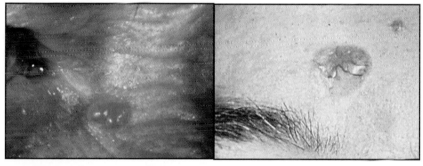

D27. Basal Cell Carcinoma (BCC)
Skin-coloured papule or plaque with rolled, translucent/pearly, telangiectatic outer border.

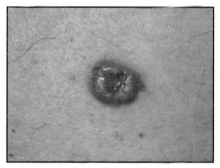

D28. Basal Cell Carcinoma
(Courtesy Dr. S. Walsh)

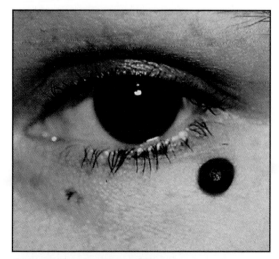

D29. Benign Compound Nevus
Proliferation of nevomelanocytes characterized by hyperpigmented macules or papules of regular shape and uniform colour.

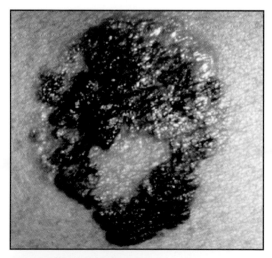

D30. Malignant Melanoma
Superficial spreading lesion characterized by asymmetrical irregular border, variegated colour, and diameter greater than 0.6 mm.

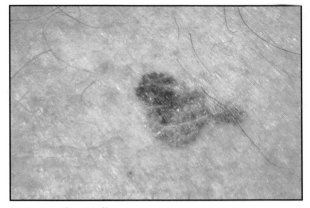

D31. Lentigo Maligna
Tan/brown uniformly flat macule with irregular borders
(Courtesy Dr. S. Walsh)

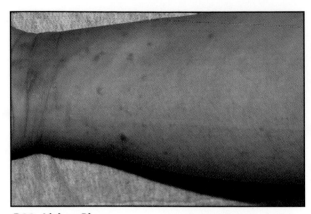

D32. Lichen Planus
Flat-topped papules with irregular, angulated borders.
Close inspection shows a lacy, reticular pattern of whitish
lines (Wickham's striae).
(Courtesy Dr. S. Walsh)

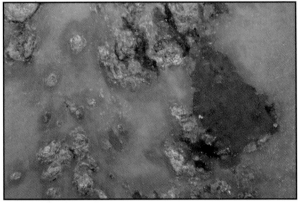

D33. Pemphigus Vulgaris
Flaccid vesicles and bullae that easily rupture; erosions
and crusts.
(Courtesy Dr. S. Walsh)

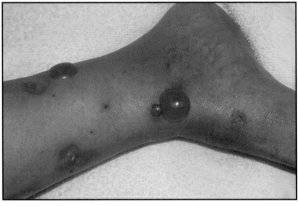

D34. Bullous Pemphigoid
Multiple tense serous and partially hemorrhagic bullae;
postinflammatory tan discoloration is present at sites of
prior erythematous urticarial-type lesions.
(Courtesy Dr. S. Walsh)

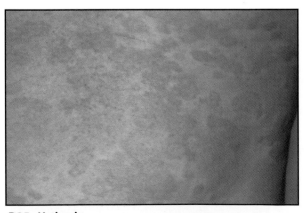

D35. Urticaria
Circumscribed, raised, edematous, red plaques surround-
ed by a faint white halo. *(Courtesy Dr. S. Walsh)*

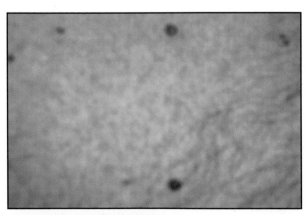

D36. Senile Hemangioma
Bright red, dome-shaped vascular papules with a 1-5 mm
diameter.

Diagnostic Medical Imaging

Approach to the Plain chest film

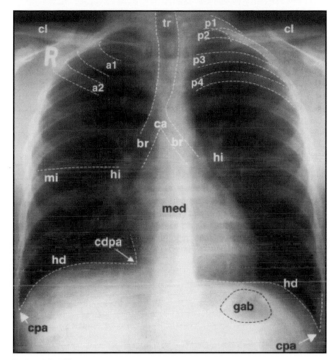

DM1. PA Film
Normal PA film of a male. Note the right and left clavicles (cl), posterior (p1-4) and anterior (a1-2) ribs, right and left costophrenic angles (cpa), right cardiophrenic angle (cdpa), right and left hemidiaphragms (hd), gastric air bubble (gab), trachea (tr), right and left mainstem bronchi (br), mediastinal shadow (med), carina (ca), and right and left hila (hi). The normal position of the minor fissure (mi) is also indicated.

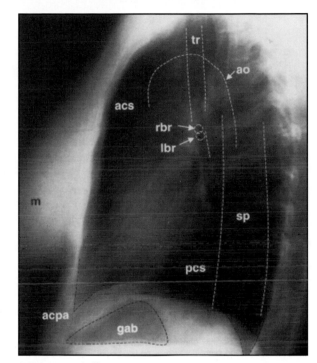

DM2. Lateral Film
This is a normal lateral film of a female patient. Note the spine (sp), anterior costophrenic angle (acpa), gastric air bubble (gab), trachea (tr), left mainstem bronchus (lbr), right mainstem bronchus (rbr), aortic arch (ao), anterior/retrosternal (acs) and posterior/ retrocardiac (pcs) clear spaces, and breast shadow (m).

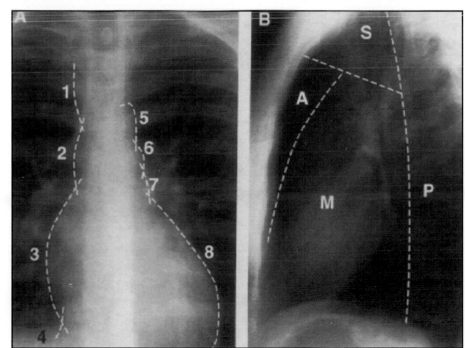

DM3. Mediastinum
Components of the PA mediastinal shadow (A) include SVC (1), ascending aorta (2), RA (3), IVC (4), aortic arch (5), pulmonary trunk (6), LA appendage (7), and LV (8). Mediastinal compartments on the lateral film (B) include: superior (S), anterior (A), middle (M) and posterior (P) compartments.

This is a useful mnemonic to remember the proper steps in examining the chest x-ray.
"It may prove quite right, but stop and be certain how lungs appear".

Identification: date of exam, patient name, sex, age
Markers: R and/or L
Position: medial ends of clavicles should be equidistant from spinous process at midline
Quality: degree of penetration (e.g., thoracic spine should be just visible through heart), lack of motion artefact
Respiration: right hemidiaphragm at 6th anterior interspace or 10th rib posteriorly on good inspiration;
poor inspiration results in poor aeration, vascular crowding, compression and widening of central shadow
Soft tissues: neck, axillae, pectoral muscles, breasts/nipples, chest wall;
nipple markers can help identify nipples (which may mimic lung nodules), observe volume of soft tissue present
Abdomen (please see Abdominal Imaging)
Bones: C-spine, T-spine, shoulder girdle, ribs, sternum (seen best on lateral film)
Central shadow: trachea, heart, great vessels, mediastinum, spine
Hila: pulmonary vessels, mainstem and segmental bronchi, lymph nodes
Lungs: lung parenchyma, pleura, diaphragm
Absent structures: review the above, noting ribs, breasts, lung lobes

Respiration

On a film taken in full inspiration, the right hemidiaphragm should project over the 6th anterior interspace or
10th rib posteriorly. Films taken without a full inspiration are described as having a "poor inspiratory result".
This may result from a poor inspiratory effort or any other condition that prevents full inspiration. This patient's
chest x-ray is normal in full inspiration. In relative expiration, the cardiac silhouette appears enlarged and the
pulmonary vasculature appears crowded and indistinct. This appearance is easily mistaken for pulmonary
edema.

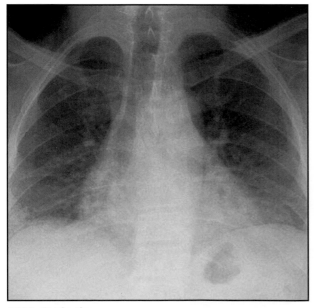

DM4. Expiration

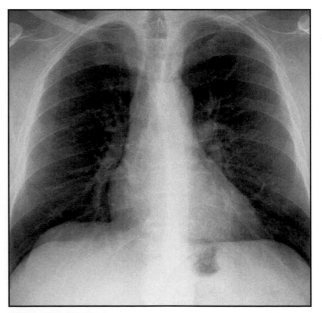

DM5. Inspiration

Soft Tissue

Nipple shadows can often mimic pulmonary nodules. Clues to the nipples being the source of the apparent nodules are positioning of the nodules on the lateral radiograph, bilaterality and "lesions" whose inferior and lateral borders appear sharper than their superior and medial margins. Confirmation can be obtained by repeating the study with nipple markers or obtaining a different projection.

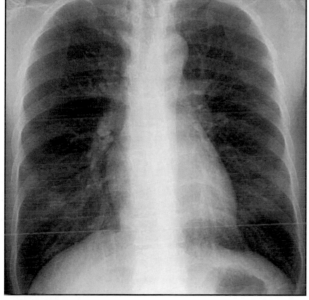

DM6. Nipple

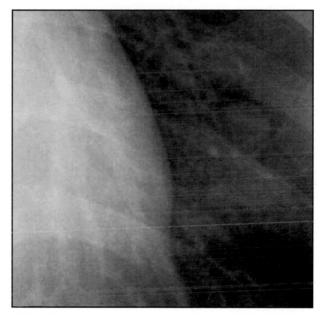

DM7. Nipple

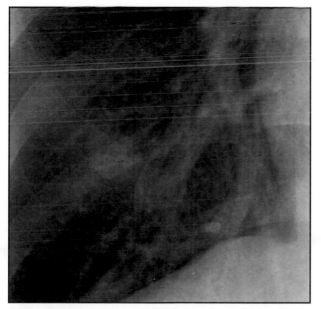

DM8. Nipple

Bone/Central Shadow

This young patient has left lower lobe pneumonia. The left hemidiaphragm is "silhouetted" by consolidation in the left lower lobe (note that one cannot see the entire left hemidiaphragm through the cardiac shadow). In a normal chest X-ray, the diaphragm and mediastinal structures are visible because of the difference in radiodensity between lung and these structures (i.e., there is an "interface" between the tissues). The silhouette sign refers to loss of normally appearing interfaces, implying opacification due to consolidation (most common), atelectasis, mass, etc., in adjacent lung.

The lateral film demonstrates the "spine sign". On a normal lateral chest X-ray, as one moves down the thoracic vertebral column, the vertebral bodies appear progressively blacker. Here they appear more radioopaque due to consolidation in the overlying left lower lobe.

DM9. Silhouette and Spine Sign

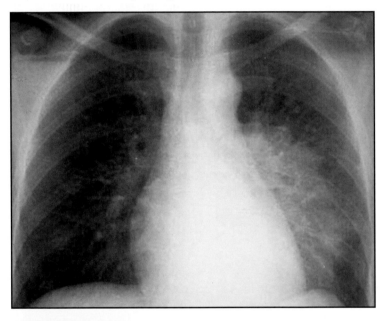

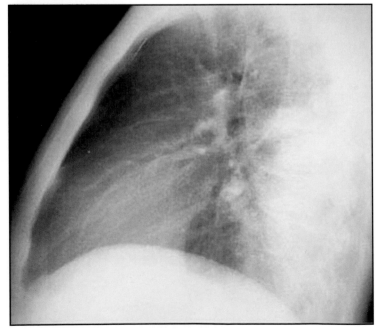

Central Shadow

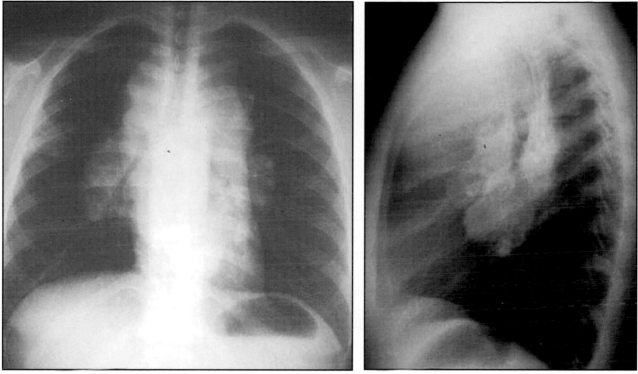

DM10. Anterior Mediastinum

There is a large mass in this patient's anterior mediastinum. In this case, the mass is accompanied by significant hilar and paratracheal lymphadenopathy. The patient is young and complains of fevers and night sweats. He was diagnosed with Hodgkin's Lymphoma.

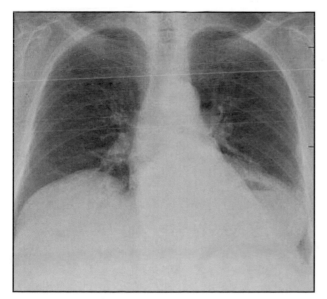

DM11. Middle Mediastinum

This patient has a large mass in the middle mediastinum.

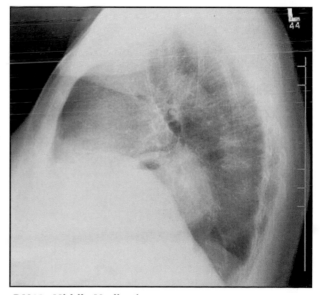

DM12. Middle Mediastinum

This elderly patient complained of gastroesophageal reflux symptoms. This clinical history, plus the presence of an air-fluid level within the mass suggests a hiatus hernia.

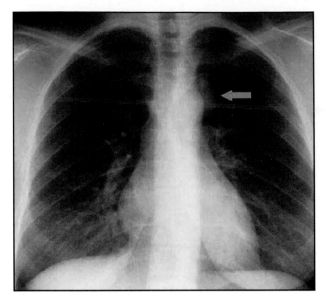

DM13. Posterior Mediastinum

This patient has a well circumscribed mass in the posterior mediastinum. The value of the lateral view is well illustrated in this case; on the frontal radiograph there is no way to localize the lesion. This mass proved to be a neurofibroma.

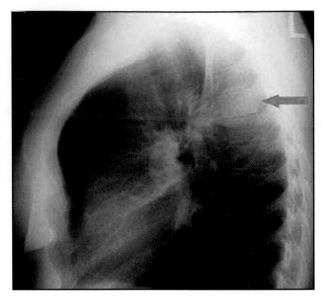

DM14. Posterior Mediastinum

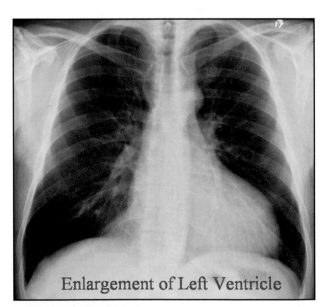

Enlargement of Left Ventricle

DM15. LV Enlargement

Evidence of an enlarged left ventricle can be as follows:
a) displacement of cardiac apex inferiorly and posteriorly
b) boot shaped heart c) Rigler's sign (on the lateral film, from the junction of inferior vena cava (IVC) and heart at the level of the diaphragm, measure 1.8 cm posteriorly and then 1.8 cm superiorly. If the cardiac shadow extends beyond this point then LV enlargement is suggested.

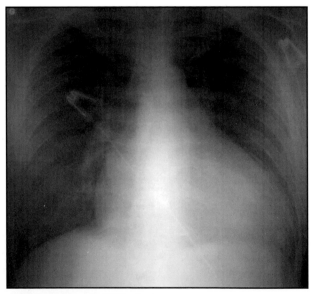

DM16. Pericardial Effusion

Evidence of a pericardial effusion can be as follows:
a) a globular heart b) loss of the indentations of the left mediastinal border c) separation of peri and epi-cardial fat pads on lateral film. The appearance is very similar to a dilated cardiomyopathy, and therefore you will need a CT scan to distinguish them.

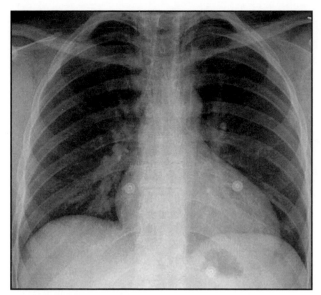

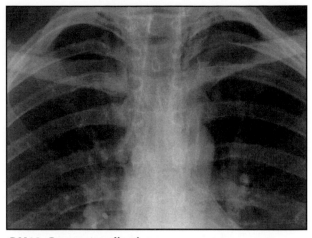

DM18. Pneumomediastinum
In the PA chest and zoomed views, note the linear lucency just superior to the left atrial shadow suggestive of a pneumomediastinum.

DM17. Pneumomediastinum
In the PA chest and zoomed views, note the linear lucency just superior to the left atrial shadow suggestive of a pneumomediastinum.

The Lungs

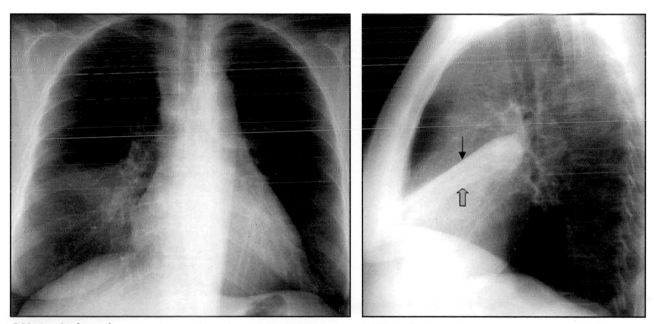

DM19a. Atelectasis
This patient has suffered complete collapse of the right middle lobe. Note the opaque, atelectatic right middle lobe projecting over the mid right hemithorax. The collapsed right middle lobe also demonstrates the "silhouette" sign; in this case, part of the adjacent right heart border is obscured by the atelectatic lobe.

DM19b. Atelectasis
The lateral view demonstrates the flat, "pancake"-shaped right middle lobe. The minor fissure (black arrow) and major fissure (green arrow) approximate as the intervening lung tissue collapses.

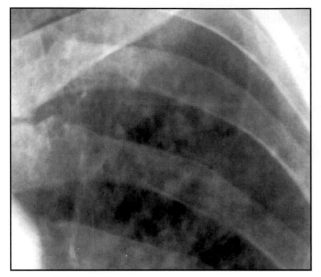

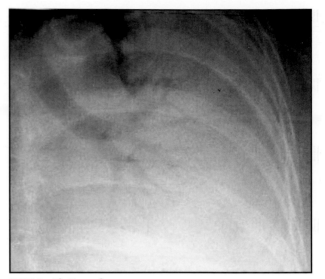

DM20. Acinar Pattern

The acinar pattern is representative of airspace disease. Seen are ill-defined, round or elliptical nodules measuring 4-8 mm. They have a characteristic "fluffy" appearance and may take on a patchy distribution, with a later tendency to coalesce into a lobar or segmental distribution.

DM21. Air Bronchogram

The air bronchograms seen in this chest X-ray represent lucent branching bronchi visible through surrounding (opaque) airspace disease.

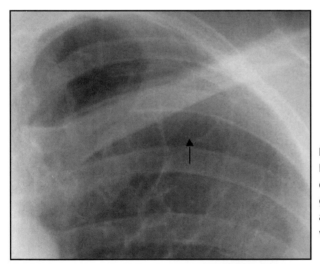

DM22. Bullae

Bullae are often associated with emphysema. By definition, a bulla is a gas-containing, avascular area of lung at least 1 cm in diameter and with a wall thickness of at least 1 mm.

DM23. Hyperinflation

This young patient has emphysema as a result of alpha-1-antitrypsin deficiency. Hyperinflation is noted as a generalized increase in radiolucency due to increased aeration and spread of vasculature, an increased AP chest diameter and retrosternal airspace on the lateral view, and diaphragmatic domes projecting well below the normal level of the 10th rib posteriorly and the 6th rib anteriorly on the PA view.

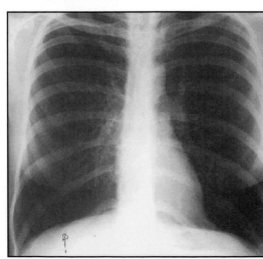

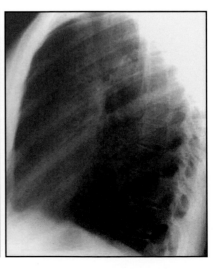

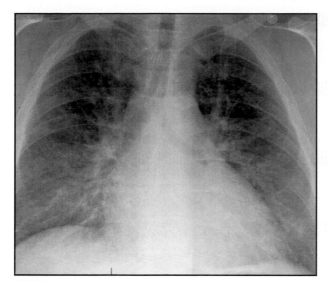

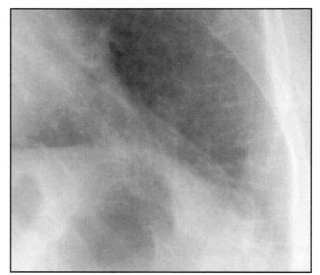

DM24a.

DM24b.

DM24. Kerley B Lines

Kerley B lines are short (1-2 cm), horizontal, linear opacities that meet the pleura at right angles. They are typically visualized at the periphery of the lower lung fields.

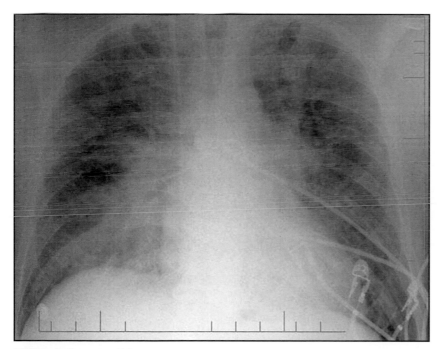

DM25. Pulmonary Edema

The plain AP films of this patient exemplify pulmonary edema. One can easily appreciate the fluffy white opacities throughout the lung field. Other signs such as vascular redistribution, peri-bronchial cuffing, and pleural effusion are difficult to appreciate on this study. However, Kerley B lines are seen, especially in the lower right lung field.

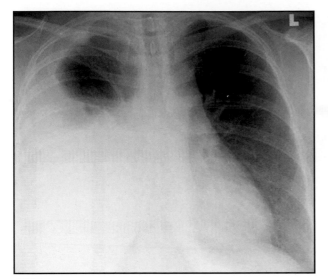

DM26a.

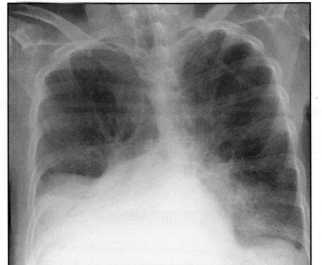

DM26b.

DM26. Pleural Effusion (PA)

In this patient, a large pleural effusion obscures most of the right lung field. In an uncomplicated effusion such as this, fluid is higher laterally than medially, forming a meniscus with the pleura. A horizontal fluid level is seen only in hydropneumothorax (both fluid and air within pleural cavity). Blunting of costophrenic angles is first noted on the PA view with approximately 200 cc of fluid accumulation.

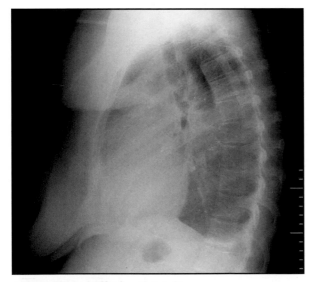

DM27. Pleural Effusion (lateral)

A small pleural effusion is noted as a blunting of the left posterior costophrenic angle. As an effusion develops, pooling of fluid occurs first in posterior recess, then spreads laterally and anteriorly; therefore the lateral film is most sensitive for pleural effusion. Blunting of the posterior costophrenic angle is first noted with a fluid accumulation of approximately 75 cc.

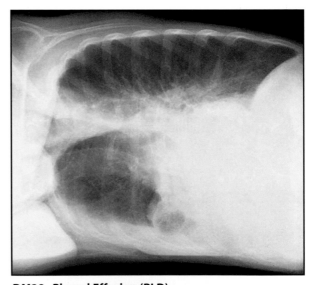

DM28. Pleural Effusion (RLD)

This patient has a moderate-sized right pleural effusion. The lateral decubitus film places the effusion in the dependent position and will show layering unless the effusion is loculated. This is noted in the same patient's left lateral decubitus film.

Reticular and Honeycomb Appearances

The reticular appearance refers to a collection of innumerable small linear opacities that together produce an appearance resembling a "net". The pattern can be fine, medium or coarse. Fine and medium patterns are shown here. Reticular patterns represent interstitial lung disease. End stage interstitial lung disease can result in the so-called "honeycomb" appearance. The honeycomb appearance is due to shadows of air spaces 5-10mm in diameter and 2-3 mm in wall thickness.

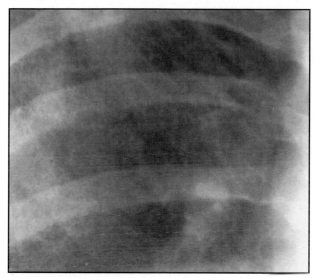

DM29. Reticular & Honeycomb (fine)

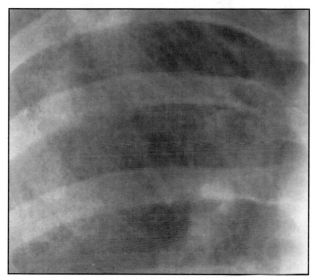

DM30. Reticular & Honeycomb (medium)

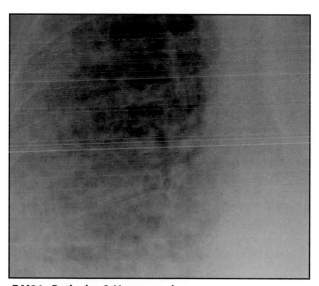

DM31. Reticular & Honeycomb

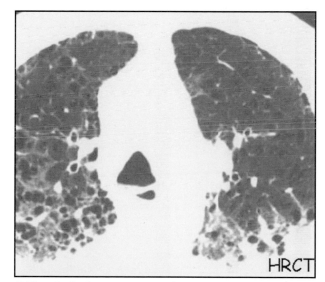

DM32. Reticular & Honeycomb

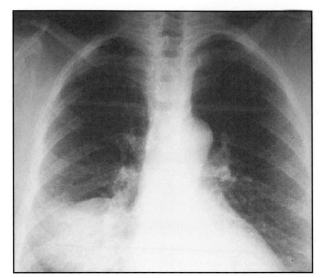

DM33a. Silhouette Sign

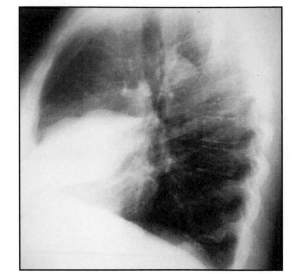

DM33b. Silhouette Sign

DM33. Silhouette Sign
The silhouette sign refers to loss of normally appearing interfaces, implying opacification due to consolidation (most common), atelectasis, mass, etc., in adjacent lung.
This patient demonstrates silhouetting of the right heart border to right middle lobe consolidation.

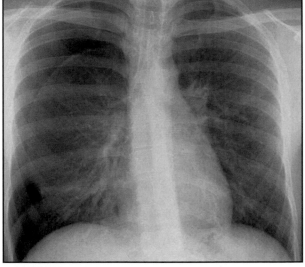

DM34. Simple Pneumothorax
There is an obvious right pneumothorax. Note the lack of vascularity in the periphery in the right hemithorax.

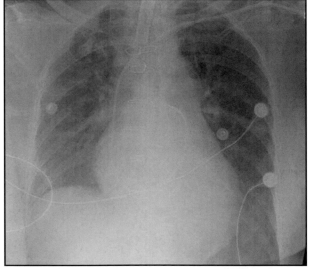

DM35. Simple Pneumothorax
The patient's left pneumothorax is more difficult to diagnose on this supine film. This study demonstrates the "deep sulcus sign", with the left costophrenic sulcus descending below the edge of the film. Other clues include a hyperlucent left hemithorax and slight sharpening of the left mediastinal border.

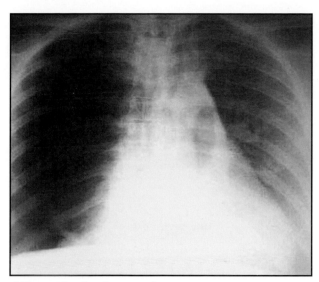

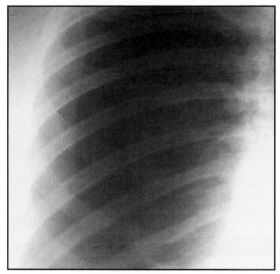

DM36a. Tension Pneumothorax

DM36b. Tension Pneumothorax

DM36. Tension Pneumothorax

In addition to the features of an uncomplicated pneumothorax, note the marked mediastinal shift to the left in this young patient with a right tension pneumothorax.

Common Clinical Scenarios in Chest Radiology

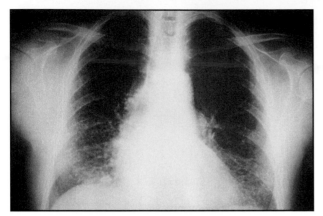

DM37. Interstitial Disease
Diffuse reticulonodular markings prominent in the lower
lung zones; linear strands and spherical densities.
(Courtesy Dr. M. Hutcheon)

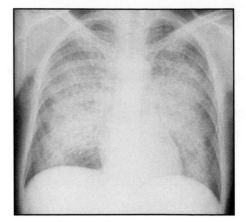

DM38. Airspace Disease
Ill-defined fluffy structures with confluences
+/− air bronchograms.
(Courtesy Dr. M. Hutcheon)

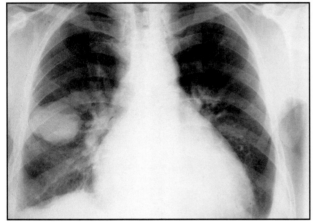

DM39. Congestive Heart Failure (CHF) (PA film)
Cardiomegaly, pulmonary congestion, blunting of costophrenic
angles, and loculated pleural effusion (pulmonary pseudotumour).

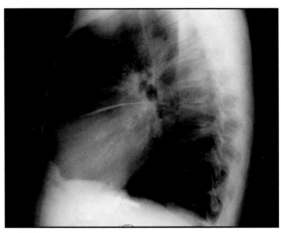

DM40. Congestive Heart Failure (CHF) (Lateral film)
Post-treatment for CHF. Note scant effusion within
fissure lines.

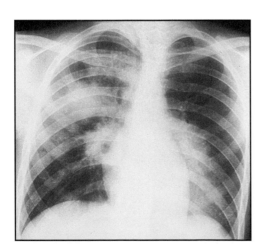

DM41. Wegener's Granulomatosis
Patchy alveolar infiltrates, widely distributed
multiple irregular masses ± pleural effusion and
± thick-walled cavities. *(Courtesy Dr. M. Hutcheon)*

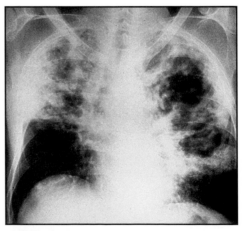

DM42. Active Tuberculosis
Cavitation in apical regions and posterior
segments of upper lobe ± calcification.
(Courtesy Dr. M. Hutcheon)

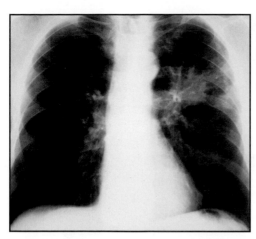

DM43. Bronchogenic Carcinoma
Ill-defined infiltrating lesion in left hilar region.

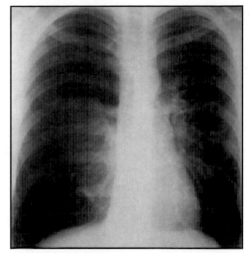

DM44. Pneumothorax
Separation of visceral and parietal pleura. Note hyperlucent lung field and small, deflated lung on right with lack of peripheral lung markings.
(Courtesy Dr. G. Olscamp)

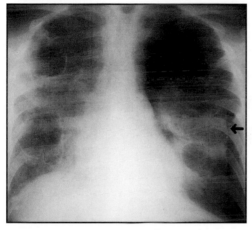

DM45. *Pneumocystis carinii* Pneumonia
Bilateral interstitial and alveolar infiltrates with typical sparing of apices. Arrow showing pneumothorax.

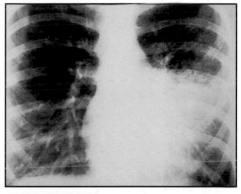

DM46. Bacterial Pneumonia
"Silhouette sign" (loss of normally appearing profiles). Unilateral localized infiltrate involving lingula and obliterating left heart border.

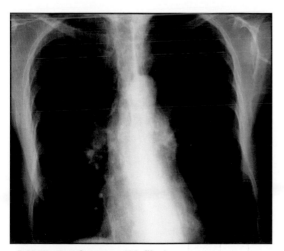

DM47. Emphysema (PA film)
Hyperinflation, darkened lung fields, and decreased vascular markings.

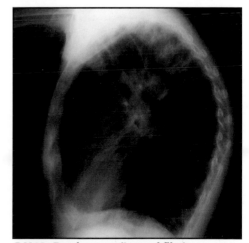

DM48. Emphysema (Lateral film)
Large retrosternal airspace, increased AP diameter (barrel chest), flattened hemi-diaphragms.

Musculoskeletal Imaging

An Approach to Fractures

Generally you should image the limbs bilaterally (unaffected and affected), image joints immediately proximal and distal to the affected joint, take AP and lateral views (and special views depending on the joint, i.e. skyline for knee or transcapular for shoulder) and then image before and after the reduction.

Site: Identify which bone, region of bone (proximal, distal, metaphyseal, etc.), intra- or extra-articular. Look for radiolucent (dark on x-ray) lines, discontinuities in the contour of the cortex.

Type: Transverse, oblique, spiral, comminuted.

Displacement: Undisplaced or displaced (angulated, translated, rotated, shortened, impaction).

Soft Tissue involvement: Calcification, gas, foreign bodies, open vs. closed. You may see features if fracture is not obvious, such as soft tissue swelling, changes in fat stripes, joint effusions and fat fluid levels caused by the displacement of periarticular fat by joint fluid.

Joints: Are the articular surfaces in apposition? Radiolucent lines? Arthritis features?

A negative x-ray does not exclude a fracture (especially in scaphoid, radial head or metatarsal head). Diagnosis is often clinical and not confirmed until 7-10 days later when enough bone resorption has occurred.

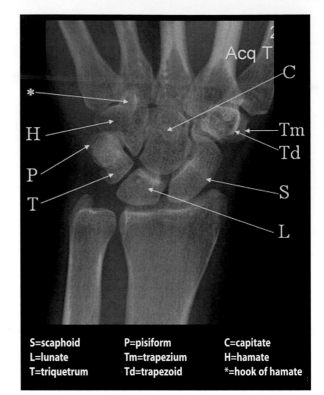

S=scaphoid	P=pisiform	C=capitate
L=lunate	Tm=trapezium	H=hamate
T=triquetrum	Td=trapezoid	*=hook of hamate

DM49. Carpal Anatomy

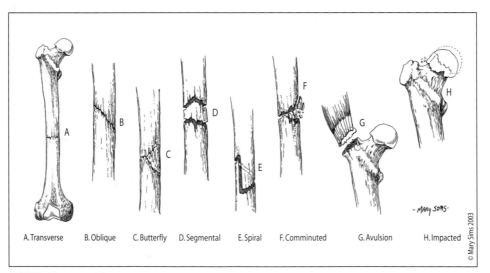

A. Transverse B. Oblique C. Butterfly D. Segmental E. Spiral F. Comminuted G. Avulsion H. Impacted

© Mary Sims 2003

DM50. Fracture Types

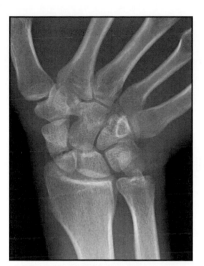

DM51. Scaphoid Fracture
The most common carpal fracture. Look for tenderness at the anatomic snuff box. Wrist x-ray is often negative.

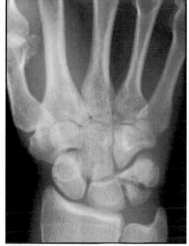

DM52. Triquetral Fracture
It is either a dorsal avulsion or body fracture. Look for tenderness dorsally, distal to ulnar styloid.

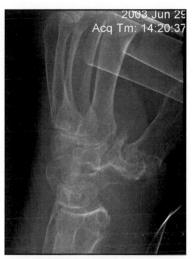

DM53. Colles and Metacarpal Fracture
Fracture of distal radius (in this case, also metacarpal), ulnar styloid, and dorsally displaced causing a dinner-fork deformity. If it is volarly displaced, it is a Smith's fracture.

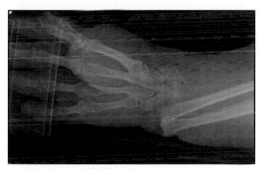

DM54. Try to find the fracture

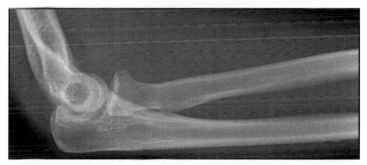

DM55. Elbow Fracture   Radial head fractures are the most common fracture of the elbow, usually resulting from fall on the outstretched hand. Pain profile includes lateral elbow tenderness and pain, and inability to fully extend the elbow.

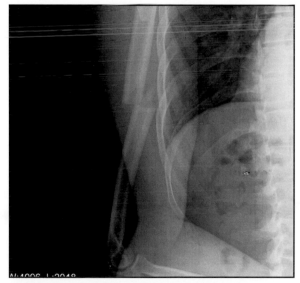

DM56. Humerus Fracture: Lateral View

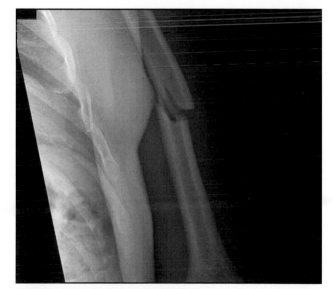

DM57. Humerus Fracture: PA View

Fractures of the proximal humerus are common in elderly with a history of osteoporosis following a FOOSH. Humerus shaft fractures (pictured here) usually occur as a result of trauma in younger patients. In this case, there is approximately 10% varus angulation, and a look at the lateral view shows anterior displacement. Clinically, look for localized pain, swelling, tenderness and shortening of the upper extremity. Radial injury is common, so look for a wrist drop.

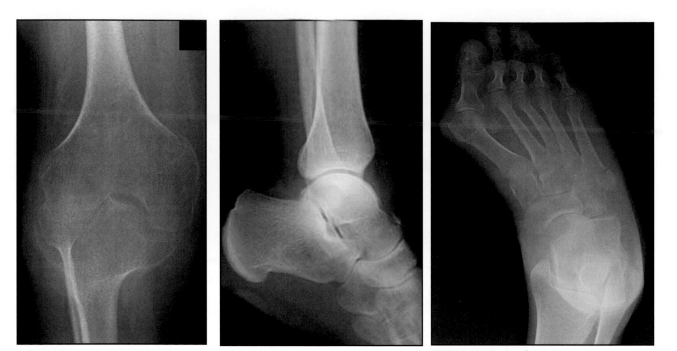

DM58. Knee; Medial Epicond   DM59. Talus Fracture   DM60. Metatarsal Fracture

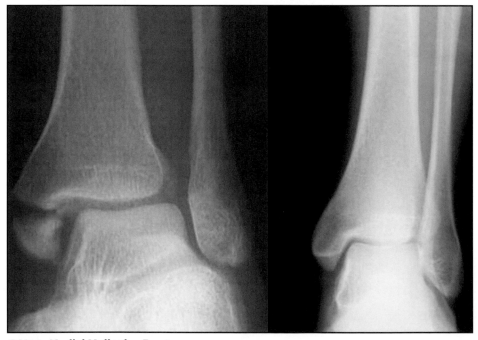

DM61. Medial Malleolus Fracture

Dislocations

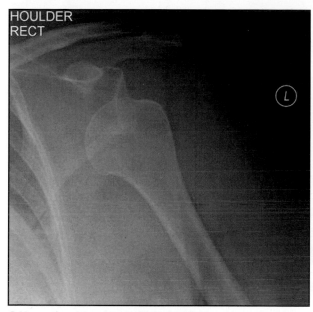

DM62. Shoulder Dislocation: PA View

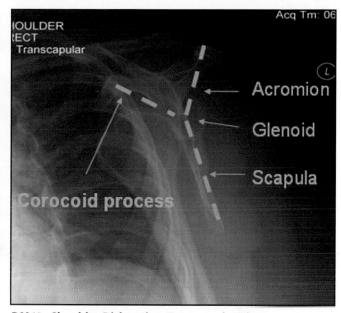

DM63. Shoulder Dislocation: Transcapular View
Mercedes-Benz sign.

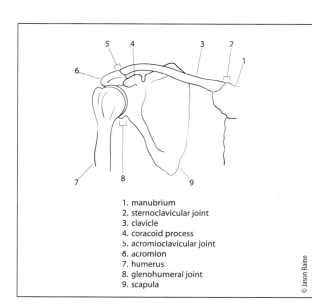

1. manubrium
2. sternoclavicular joint
3. clavicle
4. coracoid process
5. acromioclavicular joint
6. acromlon
7. humerus
8. glenohumeral joint
9. scapula

© Jason Raine

DM64. Shoulder Joints

Shoulder Dislocation

The glenohumeral joint is the most commonly dislocated joint in the body, as joint stability long ago gave way to the evolutionary requirement of joint motion. 98% of these are anterior dislocations, with posterior dislocations often missed due to poor films or physical exam. Make sure you take the appropriate views (AP, axillary lateral, transcapular). These two images show an anterior dislocation, with the humeral head anterior to the "Mercedes-Benz sign." Look for rotation by examining the tuberosity, which should appear in profile in the PA view. Also make sure to look for a Hill-Sachs lesion (a divot in the posterior humeral head), a Bankart lesion (avulsion of the glenoid labrum), rotater cuff tear, nerve injury, and stiffness.

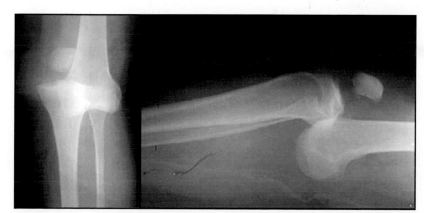

DM65. Knee Dislocation
Posterior dislocations are most common. Emergent orthopedic consult is indicated, assess neurovascular status with ABI, and arteriogram.

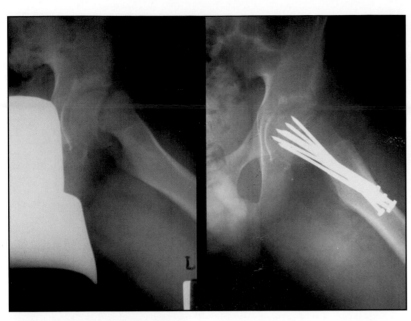

DM66. Hip Fracture
Garden IV hip fracture,
pre and post reduction.

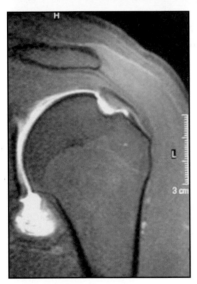

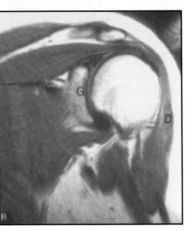

DM67. Bankart Lesion, Fracture

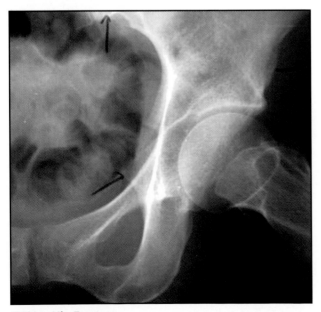

DM68. Hip Fracture

Soft Tissue Signs

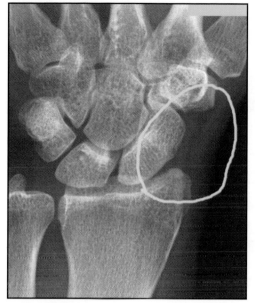

DM69. Normal X-ray.
Observe the soft tissue lines circles here, and their subsequent disruption following a scaphoid fracture.

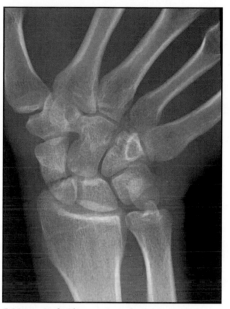

DM70. Soft Tissue; Scaphoid Fraccture

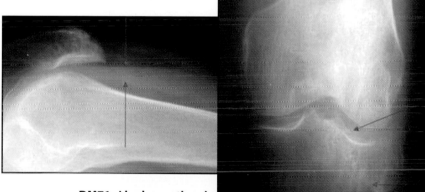

DM71. Lipohemarthrosis

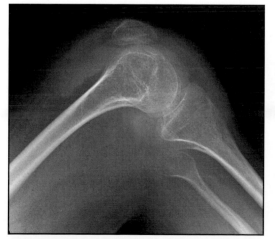

DM72. Knee Fat Fluid Level
This is indicative of a fracture, as compared to the accompanying normal image.

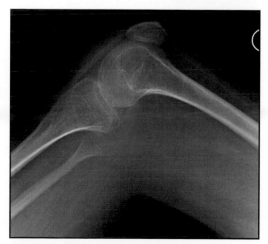

DM73. Soft Tissue; Normal Knee

Arthritis

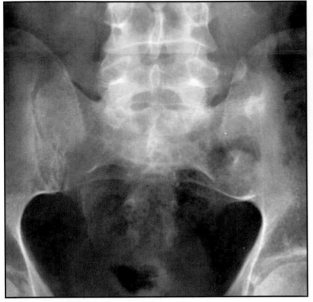

DM74. Ankylosing Spondylitis
Observe arthritic changes in the SI joint.

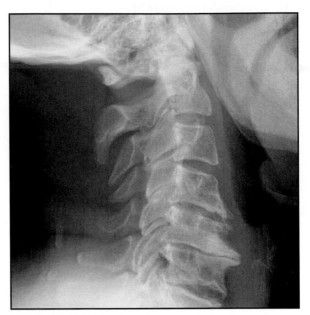

DM75. C4-5, C5-6 Severe Degeneration

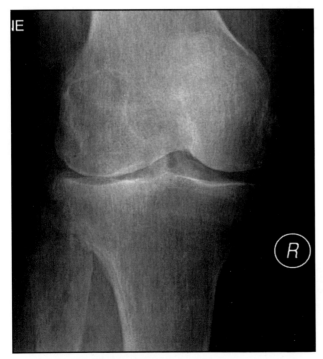

DM76. Osteoarthritis, Knee
You can see joint space narrowing, sub-chondral sclerosis, and osteophytes.

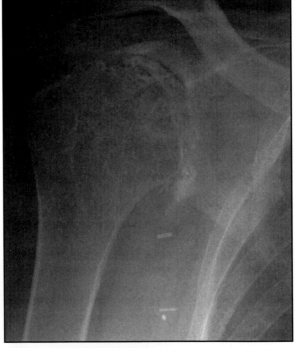

DM77. Severe Osteoarthritis

Abdominal Imaging

Gastroenterology

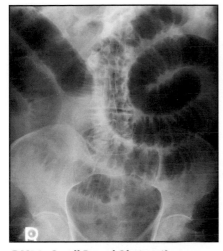

DM78. Small Bowel Obstruction
Gas in distended loops of small bowel (note plicae circularae), ladder pattern, air-fluid levels, and colon devoid of gas.

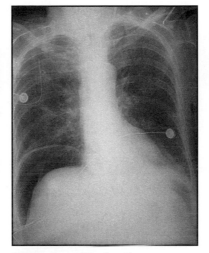

DM79. Bowel Perforation
Upright chest film showing subdiaphragmatic free air above the liver.
(Courtesy Dr. G. Olscamp)

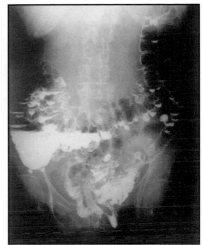

DM80. Diverticular Disease
Mucosal and submucosal herniations though muscular layer of bowel.
(Courtesy Dr. G. Olscamp)

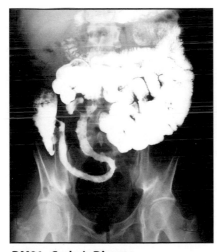

DM81. Crohn's Disease
Terminal ileitis and narrowing of the lumen due to mucosal ulceration, extensive thickening and rigidity of the bowel wall.

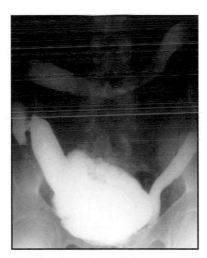

DM82. Ulcerative Colitis
Colon appears like a smooth tube due to loss of haustrations; ileocecal valve widely patent with involvement of terminal ileum.

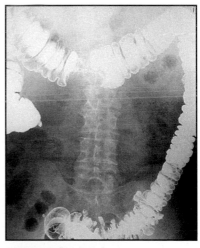

DM83. Colon Carcinoma
Classic "apple core" malignant lesion in transverse colon.
(Courtesy Dr. G. Olscamp)

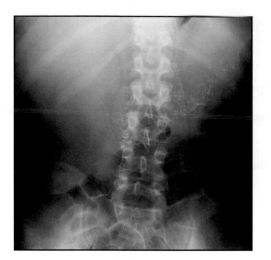

DM84. Pancreatitis
Mottled calcification in left upper quadrant suggestive of chronic pancreatitis. Note right-sided pleural effusion.

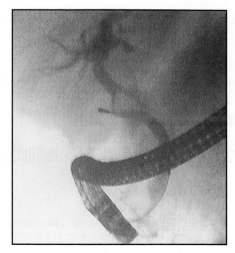

DM85. Stone in the Common Bile Duct (CBD)
Stone in the CBD just at the take-off of cystic duct.
(Courtesy Dr. G. Haber)

Abdominal Trauma

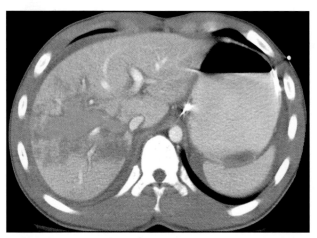

DM86. Intraparenchymal Hematoma

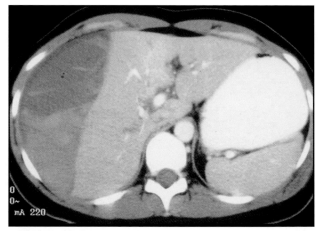

DM87. Subcapsular Hematoma

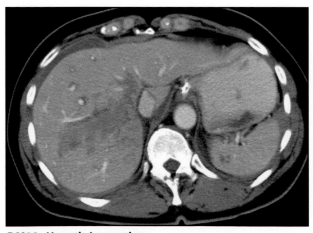

DM88. Hepatic Laceration

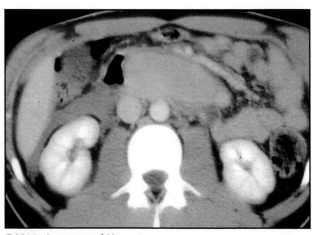

DM89. Intramural Hematoma

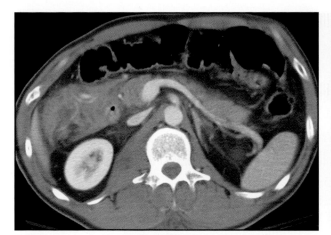

DM90. Mesenteric Hematoma

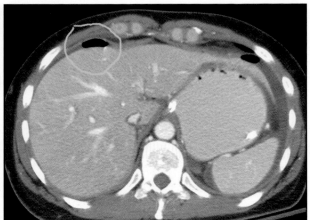

DM91. Free air from a perforation

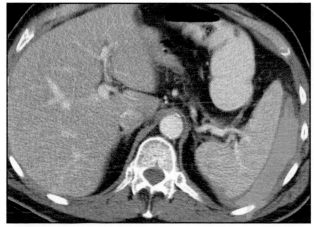

DM92. Splenic Hematoma

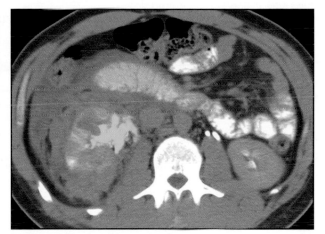

DM93. Collecting System Leak

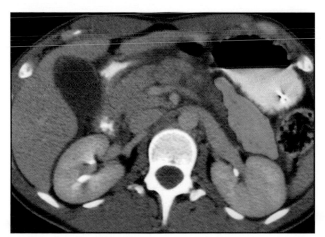

DM94. Pancreatic Laceration

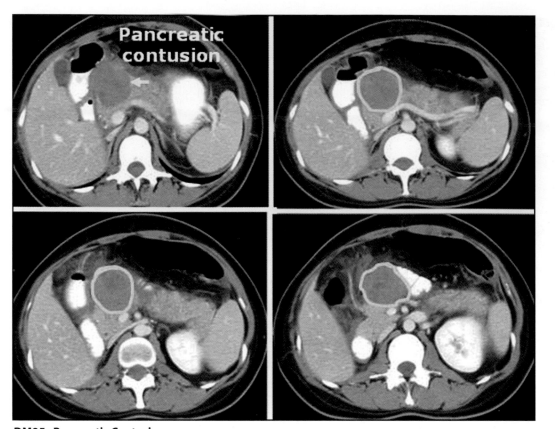

DM95. Pancreatic Contusion

Endocrinology

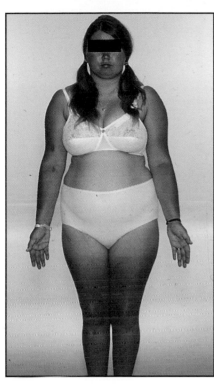

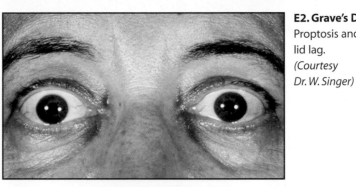

E2. Grave's Disease
Proptosis and
lid lag.
(Courtesy
Dr. W. Singer)

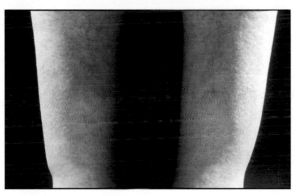

E1. Cushing's Syndrome
Note moon face, plethora, truncal obesity,
and thinning of extremeties.
(Courtesy Dr. W. Singer)

E3. Pretibial Myxedema
Waxy infiltrative plaques and edema, consistent with
infiltrative dermopathy of Grave's disease.
(Courtesy Dr. W. Singer)

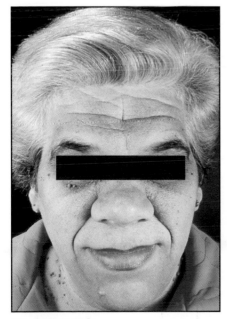

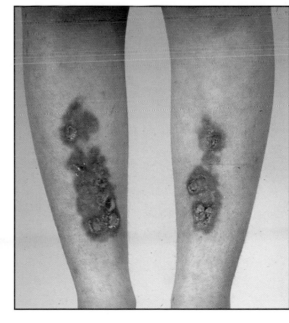

**E5. Necrobiosis
Lipoidica**
Erythematous
papules or nodules
forming shiny/waxy,
yellow-red plaques
covered with
telangectatic
vessels with scaly,
atrophic, and
depressed centre.
*(Courtesy The Hospital
for Sick Children Slide
Library, Toronto)*

E4. Acromegaly
Broad nose, thick skin, deep skin creases,
skin tags, and general coarse features.
(Courtesy Dr. W. Singer)

Gastroenterology

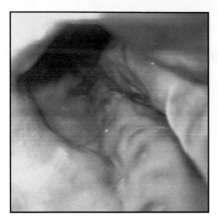

G1. Esophageal Varices
(Courtesy Dr. G. Kandel)

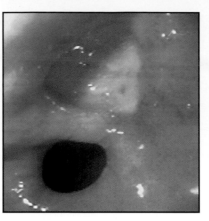

G2. Peptic Ulcer Disease
(Courtesy Dr. G. Kandel)

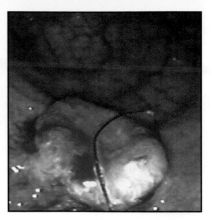

G3. Colon Carcinoma
(Courtesy Dr. G. Kandel)

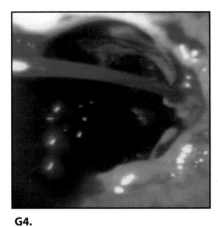

G4.
Blood spurting from a small ulcer.
(Courtesy Dr. G. Kandel)

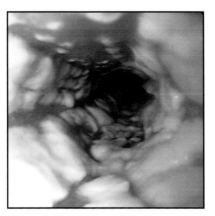

G5. Candida Esophagitis
(Courtesy Dr. G. Kandel)

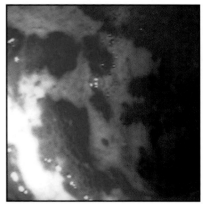

G6. Ulcerative Colitis
Diffuse, erythema, friability and loss of
normal vascular pattern.
(Courtesy Dr. G. Kandel)

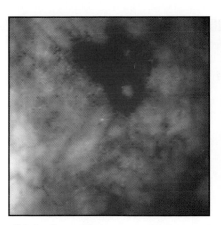

G7. Apthous Ulcer
Apthous ulcer of Crohn's disease.
Note: normal surrounding mucosa.
(Courtesy Dr. G. Kandel)

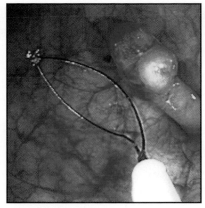

G8. Colonic Polyp
Removal with snare.
(Courtesy Dr. G. Kandel)

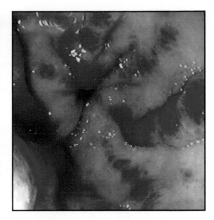

G9. Angiodysplasia
("Watermelon stomach") usually
presents as anemia, can be treated by
endoscopic coagulation.
(Courtesy Dr. G. Kandel)

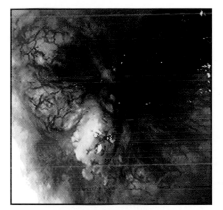

G10. Internal Hemorrhoid
As viewed by retroflexing the
colonscope.
(Courtesy Dr. G. Kandel)

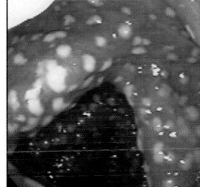

G11. Pseudomembranous Colitis
(Courtesy Dr. G. Kandel)

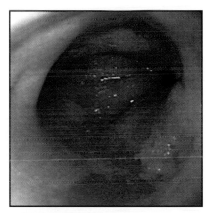

G12. Barrett's Esophagus
Short segment Barrett's
esophagus - columnar epithelium
extends up into the normal
squamous epithelium of the
esophagus in one quadrant.
(Courtesy Dr. G. Kandel)

Geriatric Medicine

Pressure Ulcer - Stage 1

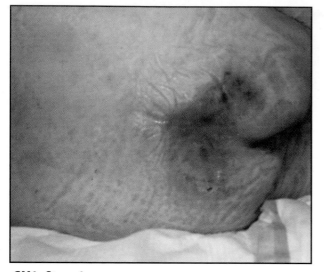

GM1. Stage 1
(Courtesy Rola Moghabghab, RN)

Pressure Ulcer - Stage 2

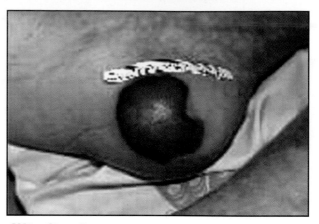

GM2a. Stage 2
(Courtesy Rola Moghabghab, RN)

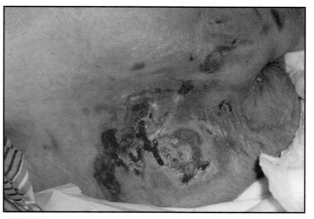

GM2b. Stage 2
(Courtesy Rola Moghabghab, RN)

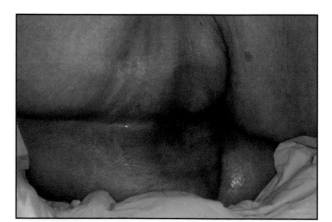

GM2c. Stage 2
(Courtesy Rola Moghabghab, RN)

Pressure Ulcer - Stage 3

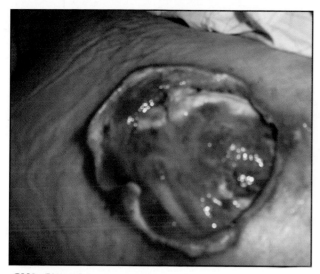

GM3. Stage 3

(Courtesy Rola Moghabghab, RN)

Pressure Ulcer - Stage 4

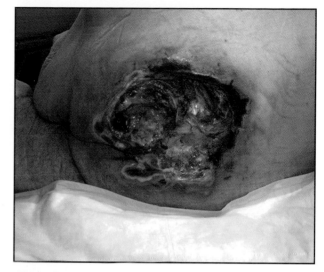

GM4a. Stage 4

(Courtesy Rola Moghabyhab, RN)

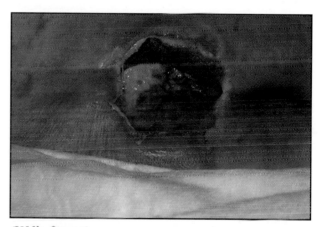

GM4b. Stage 4

(Courtesy Rola Moghabghab, RN)

Gynecology

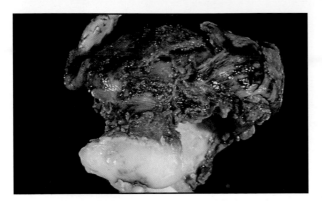

GY1. Endometriosis
Uterus with hemorrhagic fibrovascular adhesions on its serosal surface.
(Courtesy Dr. I. Zbeiranowski)

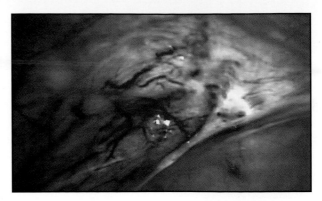

GY2. Endometriosis Laporoscopic view
Brownish-black implant on the uterosacral ligament.
(Courtesy Dr. R. Pittini)

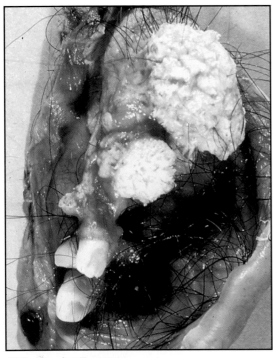

GY3. Ovarian Teratoma
Gross appearance of an ovary with a mature cystic teratoma.
(Courtesy Dr. I. Zbeiranowski)

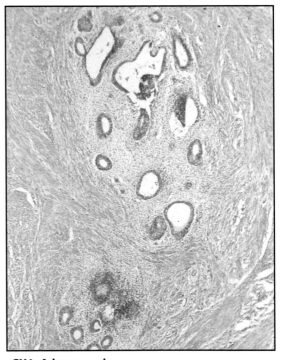

GY4. Adenomyosis
Microscopic endometrial stroma and glands present deep within myometrium.
(Courtesy Dr. I. Zbeiranowski)

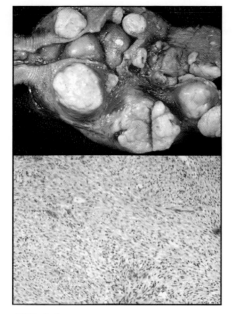

GY5. Leiomyoma
Top: Uterus with multiple leiomyomas.
Bottom: Microscopic view showing
proliferative smooth muscle cells.
(*Courtesy Dr. I. Zbeiranowski*)

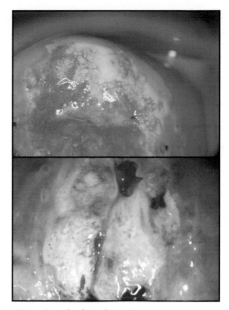

GY6. Cervical Lesion
Top: Low-grade squamous
intra-epithelial lesion stained with
acetic acid.
Bottom: Invasive cervical cancer.
(*Courtesy Dr. G. Likrish*)

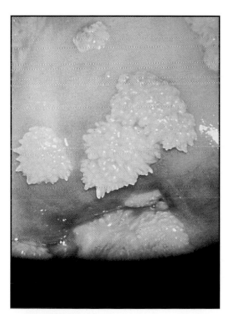

GY7. Condyloma Acuminata
("genital warts") View of the cervix.
Range from pinhead papules to soft
cauliflower-like, skin coloured masses in
clusters; associated with human papilloma
virus (HPV).
(*Courtesy Dr. W. Chapman*)

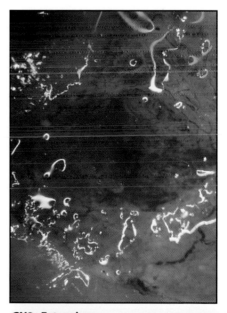

GY8. Ectropion
Eversion of cervical canal, with columnar
epithelium farther outside the external
os of the cervix.
(*Courtesy Dr. G. Likrish*)

Hematology

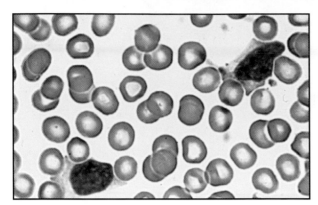

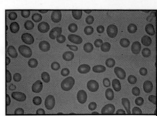

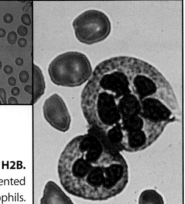

H2A. Megaloblastic Anemia
Oval macrocytes.

H2B. Hypersegmented neutrophils.

H1. Infectious Mononucleosis
Reactive large, cytoplasmic lymphocytes. Note indented cytoplasm and eccentrically placed nucleus.

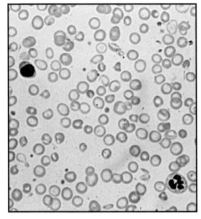

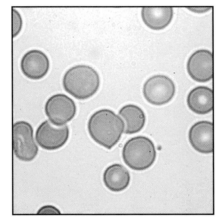

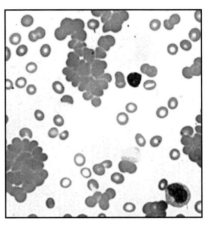

H3. Iron Deficiency Anemia
Microcytosis and hypochromia of red blood cells. Note increased area of central pallor.

H4. Hemolytic Anemia
Macrocytes and microspherocytes with polychromasia (purplish tinge).

H5. Autoimmune Hemolytic Anemia
Agglutination of red blood cells.

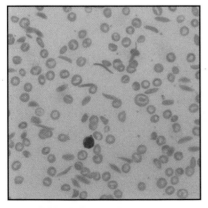

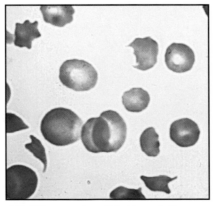

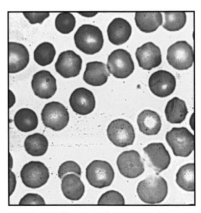

H6. Sickle Cell Anemia
Elongated, crescent-shaped and sickle red blood cells. Also note target cells and Howell-Jolly body (both due to autosplenectomy secondary to repeated splenic infarcts).
(Courtesy Dr. M. Reis)

H7. Microangiopathic Hemolytic Anemia
Fragmented red blood cells (schistocytes). Note helmet cell and triangle-shaped cell in bottom right field.

H8. Hereditary Spherocytosis
Small, round, densely staining red blood cells with no central area of pallor.

Hematologic Malignancies

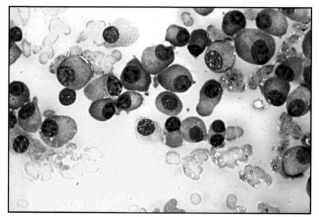

H9. Multiple Myeloma (Bone Marrow)
Plasma cells in marrow. Note binucleate malignant plasma cell in center field.

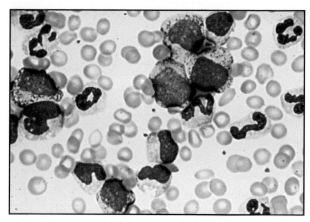

H10. Chronic Myelogenous Leukemia (CML)
Increased numbers of granulocytes and their precursors. Note most WBCs are band forms or segmented granulocytes.

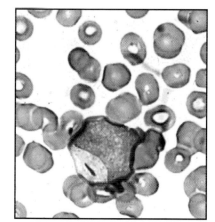

H11. Acute Myelogenous Leukemia (AML)
Note blast cell with Auer rod.

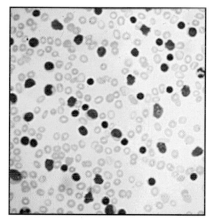

H12. Chronic Lymphocytic Leukemia (CLL) Increased number of small, well-differentiated lymphocytes. Note "smudge cells."

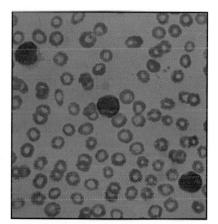

H13. Acute Lymphoblastic Leukemia (ALL) Round or convoluted nuclei, absence of cytoplasmic granules, and high nuclear to cytoplasmic ratio.
(Courtesy Dr. D. Sutton)

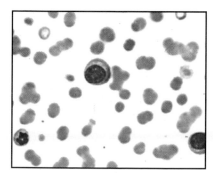

H14. Plasma Cell Myeloma
Note "rouleaux."

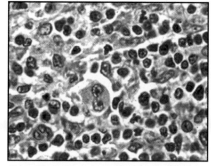

H15. Hodgkin's Lymphoma (Lymph Node) Reed-Sternberg cell is large and bilobed or binucleate. Prominent within the mirror-image nuclei are giant inclusion-like nucleoli ("owl's eyes").

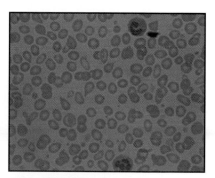

H16. Myelofibrosis
Tear drop red blood cells (poikilocytes) in the center field.
(Courtesy Dr. D. Sutton)

Infectious Diseases

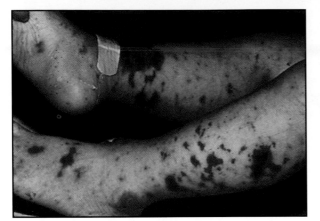

ID1. Meningococcemia

Hemorrhagic papules or petechia with purpuric centres in acral distribution.

(Courtesy The Hospital for Sick Children Slide Library, Toronto)

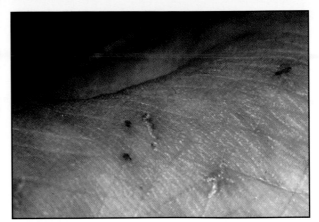
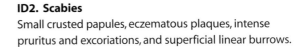

ID2. Scabies

Small crusted papules, eczematous plaques, intense pruritus and excoriations, and superficial linear burrows.

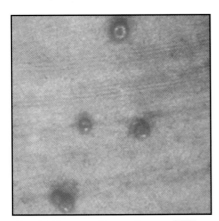

ID3. Molluscum Contagiosum

Discrete, umbilicated pearly white papules.

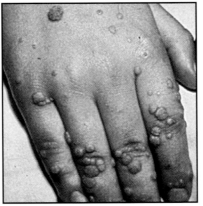

ID4. Verruca Vulgaris ("common warts")

Multiple hyperkeratotic, elevated, discrete epithelial growths with papillated surface.

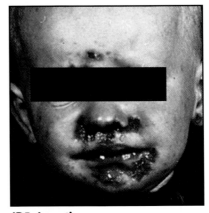

ID5. Impetigo

Honey-coloured, "stuck-on" crusts, and erythematous weeping erosions.

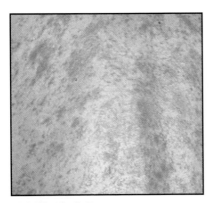

ID6. Pityriasis Rosea

Multiple round to oval erythematous patches with fine central scale.

(Courtesy Dr. L. From)

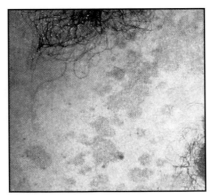

ID7. Pityriasis Versicolor

Brownish-white scaling macules on trunk.

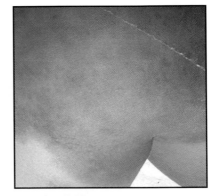

ID8. Erysipelas

Streptococcal infection of the superficial dermis consisting of sharply delineated edematous plaques with raised margins.

(Courtesy Dr. M. Mian)

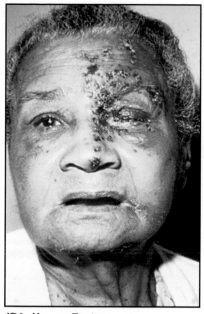

ID9. Herpes Zoster
Hemorrhagic vesicles and pustules on
an erythematous base limited to a
dermatome.
(Courtesy Dr. L. From)

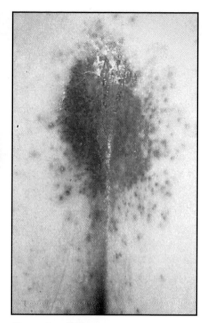

ID10. Candidiasis
Macerated or eroded erythematous
patches; often studded with papules,
pustules, and "satellite" lesions.

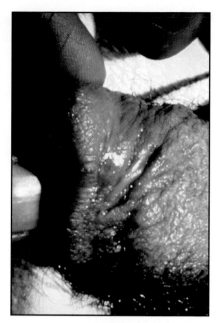

ID11. Primary Syphilis
Single, erythematous, painless round
chancre on penis.

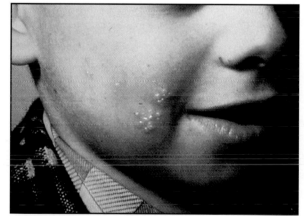

**ID12. Herpes
Simplex**
Grouped vesicular
eruption
(herpetiform
arrangement) on an
erythematous base
of skin.

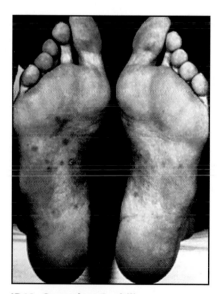

ID13. Secondary Syphilis
Commonly affecting palms and soles
with oval, flat-topped, scaling,
non-pruritic, red-brown papules.

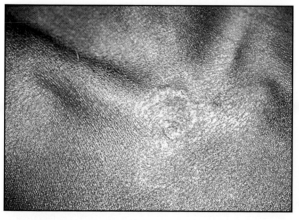

ID14. Tinea Corporis
Pruritic, scaly, round/oval plaque with central
clearing on the clavicle. *(Courtesy Dr. L. From)*

Nephrology

Interpretation of Casts

Hyaline	• Not indicative of renal disease • Concentrated urine • Fever • Exercise
RBC	• Glomerular bleeding (glomerulonephritis) = active sediment
Leukocyte	• Pyelonephritis • Interstitial nephritis
Heme-granular	• ATN • Proliferative glomerulonephritis (GN)
Fatty casts/oval fat bodies	• Nephrotic syndrome

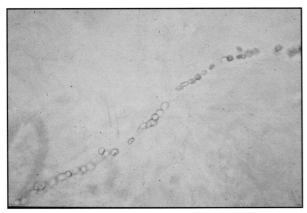

NP1. RBC Cast
Glomerular bleeding.

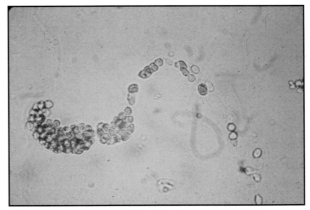

NP2. RBC Cast
Glomerular bleeding.

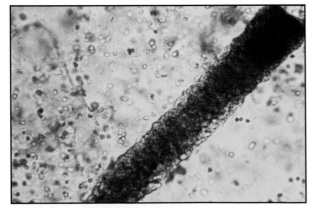

NP3. Heme-Granular Cast
Acute tubular necrosis or proliferative glomerulonephrities.

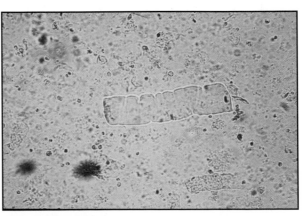

NP4. Hyaline Cast

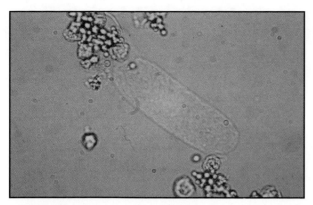

NP5. Hyaline Cast

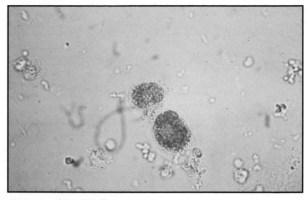

NP6. Oval Fat Bodies
Nephrotic syndrome.

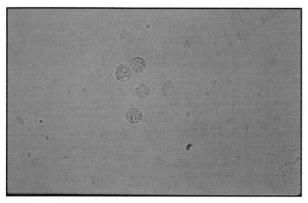

NP7. WBCs

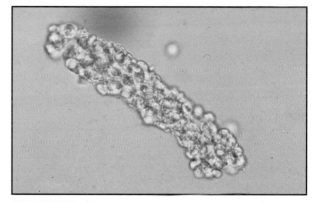

NP8. WBC Cast
Pyelonephritis or interstitial nephritis.

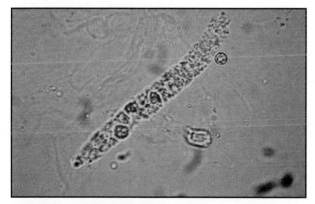

NP9. WBC and Granular Cast
Pyelonephritis or interstitial nephritis.

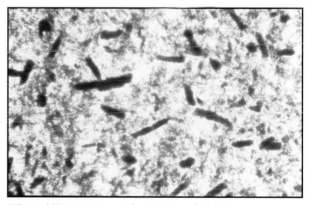

NP10. ATN: Hemegranular Casts and Debris
Acute tubular necrosis (ATN).

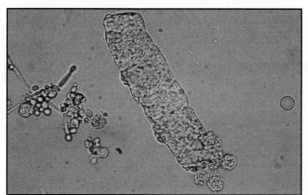

NP11. Broad Granular Cast

Neurosurgery

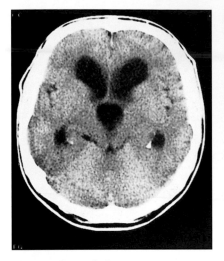

NS1. Hydrocephalus
Ventricular enlargement, periventricular lucency, narrow or absent sulci +/- fourth ventricular enlargement.

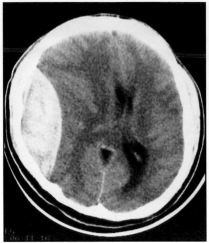

NS2. Epidural Hemorrhage
Right high density biconvex mass, usually uniform density and sharp margins.

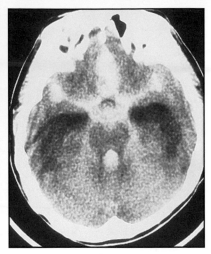

NS3. Subarachnoid Hemorrhage (SAH) CT without contrast showing blood in basal and suprasellar cisterns, interhemispheric and sylvian fissures.

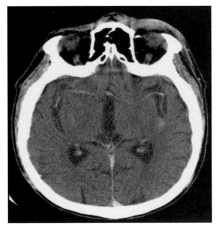

NS4. Subarachnoid Hemmorage

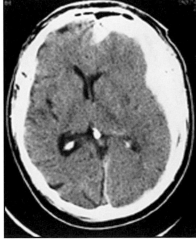

NS5. Acute Subdural Hemorrhage
Left increased density, concave mass usually less uniform, less dense, and more diffuse than epidural hemorrhage. Note compression of ventricles and midline shift.

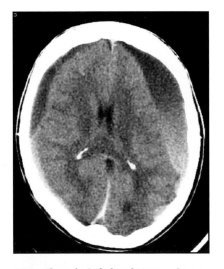

NS6. Chronic Subdural Hemorrhage
Bilateral hypodense areas representing old blood, mass effect.

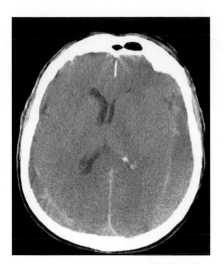

NS7. Chronic Subdural Hematoma (bilateral)
(Courtesy Dr. P. Porter)

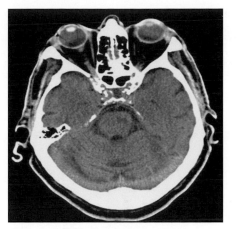

NS8. Left Pons Hypoattenuation

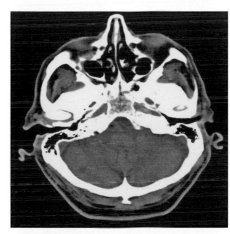

NS9. Right Posterior Fossa Lesion

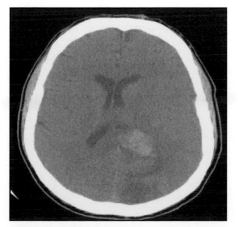

NS10. Left PCA Infarct

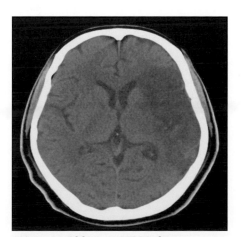

NS11. An Old Large MCA Infarct

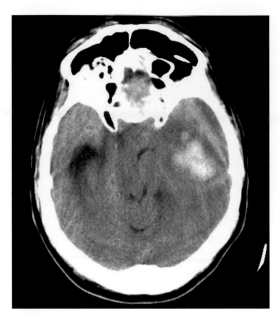

NS12. Left Temporal Contusion
Left temporal contusion with left uncal herniation.
(Courtesy Dr. P. Porter)

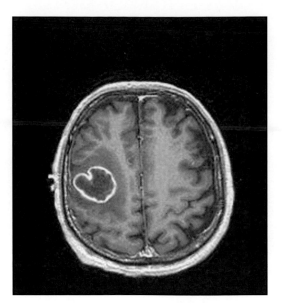

NS13. Right Frontoparietal Abscess
(Courtesy Dr. P. Porter)

NS14. Arteriovenous Malformation (AVM)
Retractor is indicating junction between arterial and
venous blood.
(Courtesy Dr. P. Porter)

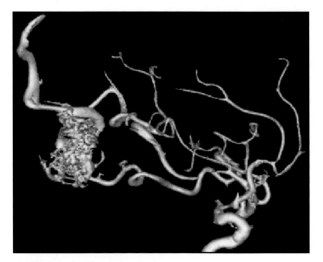

NS15. 3-D Angiogram
Arteriovenous malformation (AVM).
(Courtesy Dr. P. Porter)

NS16. Intraoperative Arteriovenous Malformation (AVM)
(Courtesy Dr. P. Porter)

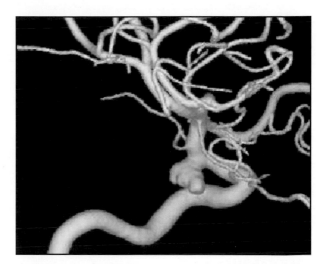

NS17. 3-D Angiogram
3-D angiogram of posterior communicating artery aneurysm.
(Courtesy Dr. P. Porter)

NS18. Angiogram of Basilar Artery Aneurysm
(Courtesy Dr. P. Porter)

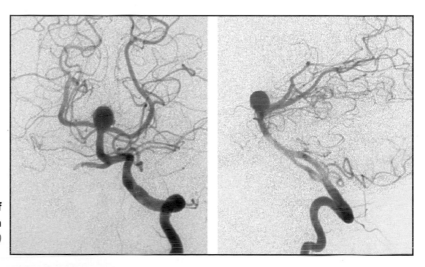

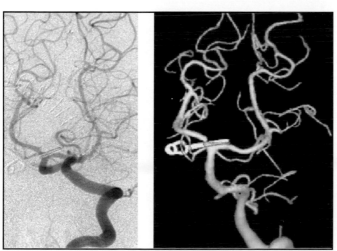

NS19. Angiograms of Basilar Artery Aneurysm Clipped
(Courtesy Dr. P. Porter)

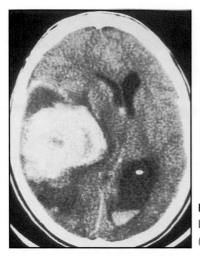

NS20. Intracranial Mass
Large glioma with midline shift and compression of sulci.
(Courtesy Dr. G. Olscamp)

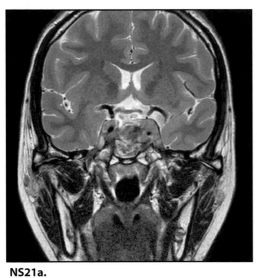

NS21a.

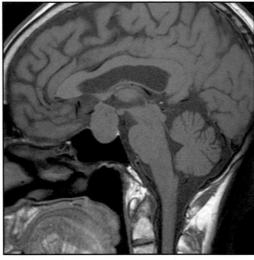

NS21b.

NS21. Pituitary Macroadenoma
(Courtesy Dr. W. Montanera)

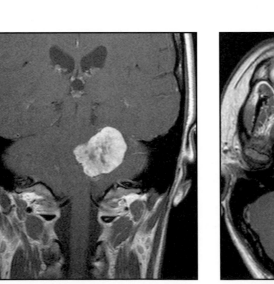

NS22a.

NS22b.

NS22. Vestibular Schwannoma
Tumour in cerebellopontine angle.
(Courtesy Dr. W. Montanera)

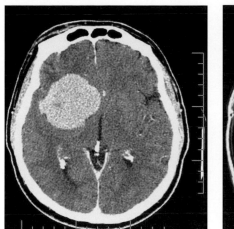

NS23a.

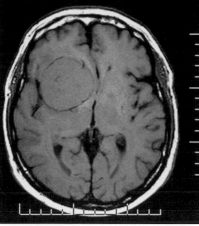

NS23b.

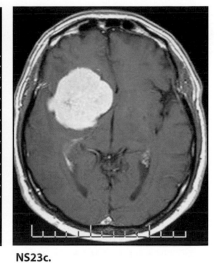

NS23c.

NS23. Meningioma
Well-demarcated, homogeneous, extra-axial lesion.
a) CT b) T1 weighted MRI (Note that the tumour is isointense to the gray matter) c) T1 weighted MRI post contrast.
(Courtesy Dr. W. Montanera)

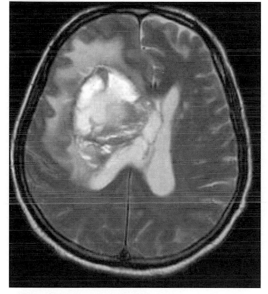

NS24. Glioblastoma Multiforme
Large inhomogeneous mass with irregular borders and associated hemorrhage.
(Courtesy Dr. W. Montanera)

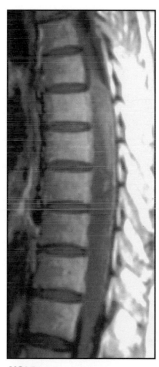

NS25a.

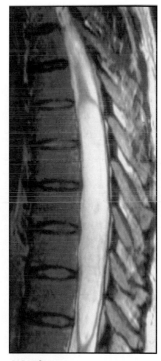

NS25b.

NS25. Astrocytoma
a) T1 and b) T2 weighted MRI of an intramedullary tumour.
(Courtesy Dr. W. Montanera)

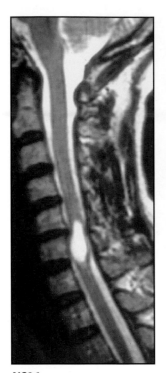

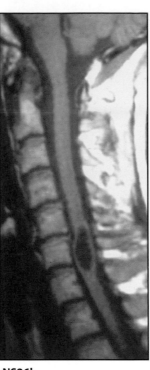

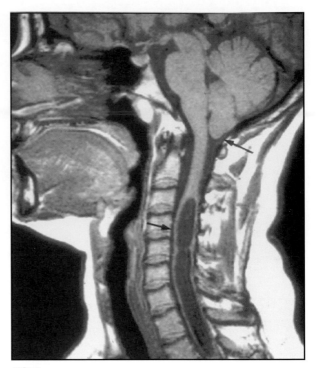

NS26a.   **NS26b.**   **NS26c.**

NS26. Syringomyelia
a) T2 weighted MRI b) T1 weighted MRI c) T1 weighted MRI of another case.
(Courtesy Dr. W. Montanera)

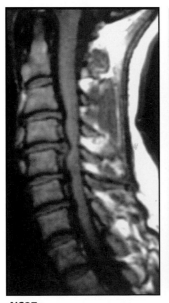

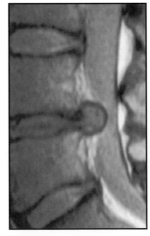

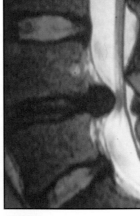

NS28a.   **NS28b.**

NS28. Disc Herniation
a) Intermediate and b) T2 weighted MRI demonstrating
large disc herniation with spinal cord compression.
(Courtesy Dr. W. Montanera)

NS27a.   **NS27b.**

NS27. Cervical Disc Herniation
a) T1 and b) T2 weighted MRI of degenerative cervical disc
herniation.
(Courtesy Dr. W. Montanera)

Obstetrics

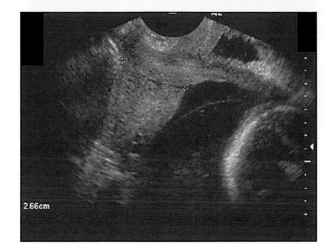

OB1. Cervix
(Courtesy of Dr. Seaward and Dr. Ryan, Fetal Medicine Unit, Mt Sinai Hospital)

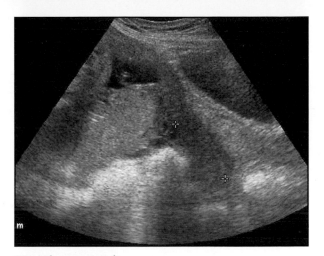

OB2. Placenta Previa
(Courtesy of Dr. Seaward and Dr. Ryan, Fetal Medicine Unit, Mt Sinai Hospital)

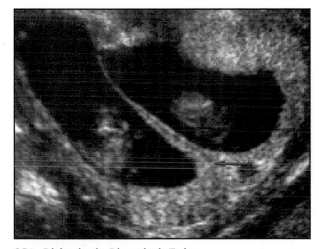

**OB3. Dichorionic, Diamniotic Twins
Lambda Sign**
(Courtesy of Dr. Seaward and Dr. Ryan, Fetal Medicine Unit, Mt Sinai Hospital)

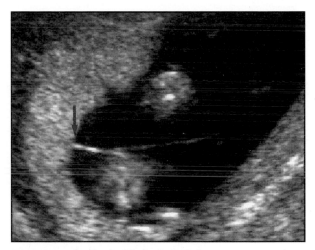

**OB4. Monochorionic, Diamniotic Twins
T Sign**
(Courtesy of Dr. Seaward and Dr. Ryan, Fetal Medicine Unit, Mt Sinai Hospital)

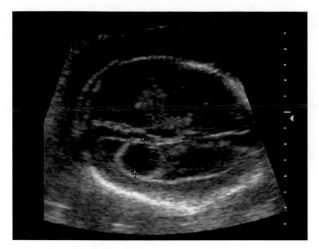

OB5. Choroid Plexus Cyst

(Courtesy of Dr. Seaward and Dr. Ryan, Fetal Medicine Unit, Mt Sinai Hospital)

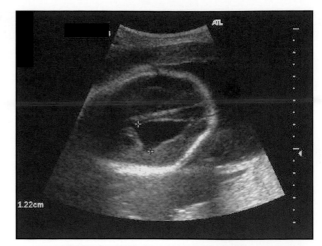

OB6. Ventriculomegaly

(Courtesy of Dr. Seaward and Dr. Ryan, Fetal Medicine Unit, Mt Sinai Hospital)

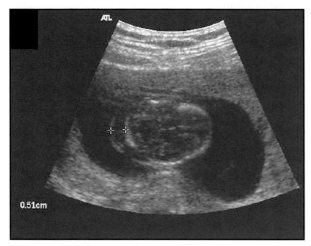

OB7. Nuchal Translucency

(Courtesy of Dr. Seaward and Dr. Ryan, Fetal Medicine Unit, Mt Sinai Hospital)

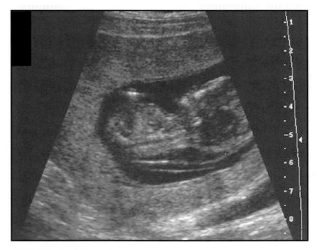

OB8. Nuchal Translucency

(Courtesy of Dr. Seaward and Dr. Ryan, Fetal Medicine Unit, Mt Sinai Hospital)

Ophthalmology

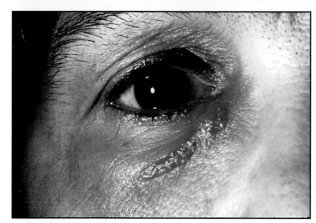

OP1. Dacryocystitis
Erythematous inflammation of the lacrimal sac.

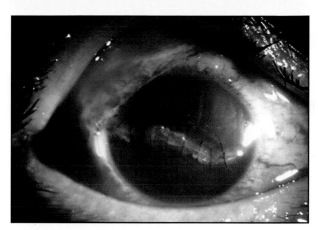

OP2. Corneal Laceration

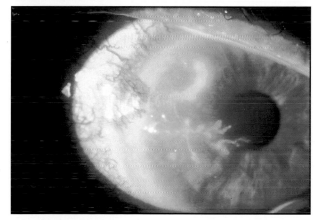

OP3. Herpes Simplex
Irregular dendritic (branch like) lesion of corneal epithelium stained with fluorescein.

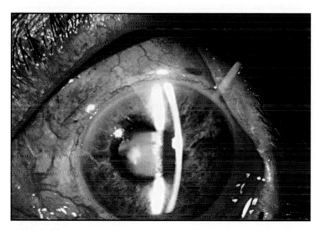

OP4. Iritis
Ciliary flush and constricted pupil.

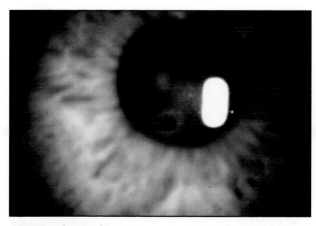

OP5. Foreign Body
Presence of rust ring on cornea after removal of metallic foreign body.

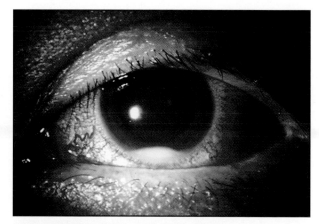

OP6. Endophthalmitis with Hypopyon
Prominent layer of purulent material in inferior aspect of anterior chamber. Note corneal edema and conjunctival injection.

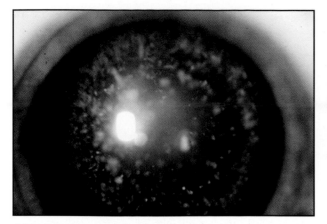

OP7. Cataract
Nuclear sclerosis with opacified lens.

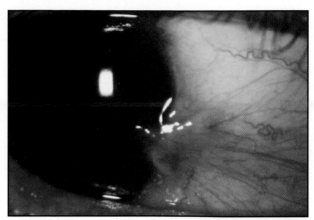

OP8. Pterygium
Pterygium extends onto the cornea
(Courtesy of Department of Ophthalmology, University of Toronto)

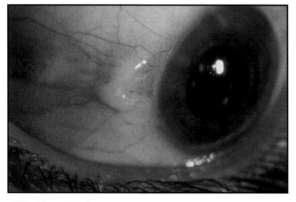

OP9. Pingueculum
Pingueculum is degenerative collagen within the interpalbebral fissure.
(Courtesy of Department of Ophthalmology, University of Toronto)

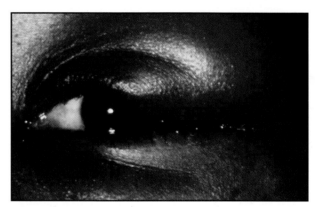

OP10. Dacryoadenitis
(Courtesy of Department of Ophthalmology, University of Toronto)

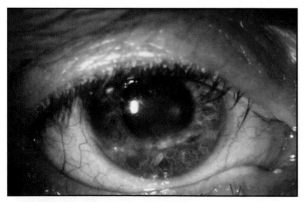

OP11. Blepharitis
Blepharitis as characterized by erythema of the lid margins and scales on the lashes.
(Courtesy of Department of Ophthalmology, University of Toronto)

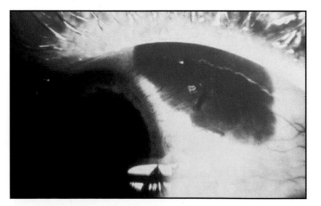

OP12. Subconjunctival Hemorrhage
Subconjunctival hemorrhage as evidenced by a bright red colour.
(Courtesy of Department of Ophthalmology, University of Toronto)

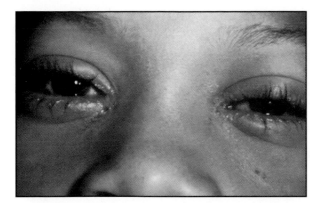

OP13. Viral Conjunctivitis
Adenoviral conjunctivitis with lid swelling, conjunctival injection and tearing.
(Courtesy of Department of Ophthalmology, University of Toronto)

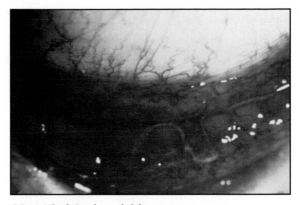

OP14. Viral Conjunctivitis
Adenoviral conjunctivitis with lid swelling, conjunctival injection and tearing.
(Courtesy of Department of Ophthalmology, University of Toronto)

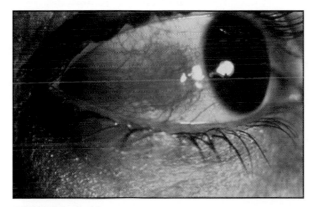

OP15. Episcleritis
Episcleritis with sectorial injection of the conjunctiva and episcleral tissue.
(Courtesy of Department of Ophthalmology, University of Toronto)

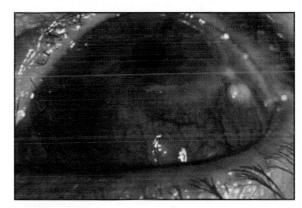

OP16. Scleritis
Scleritis with diffuse involvement on the deep episcleral vessels.
(Courtesy of Department of Ophthalmology, University of Toronto)

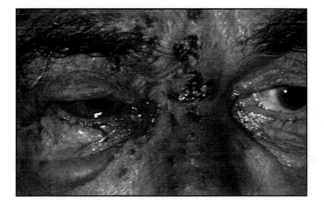

OP17. Herpes Zoster Keratitis
Herpes zoster ophthalmicus with trigeminal nerve distribution.
(Courtesy of Department of Ophthalmology, University of Toronto)

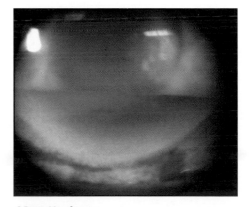

OP18. Hyphema
(Courtesy of Dr. Andrew Doan and www.eyerounds.org)

Glaucoma

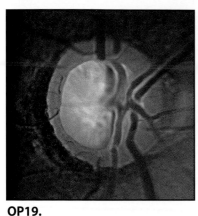

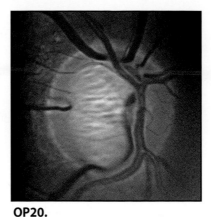

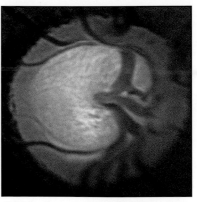

OP19.

OP20.

Optic Disc Enlargement, thinning(or notching) of neuroretinal rim usually beginning inferiorly (as in these discs), deepening of optic cup. Notching thinning of neuroretinal rim tends to occur, inferiorly, then superiorly, then temporally, and nasal is the last one to be affected.
© 2003 Dr. Yan

OP21. Concentric Enlargement of Optic Disc
Deepening of optic cup.
© 2003 Dr. Yan

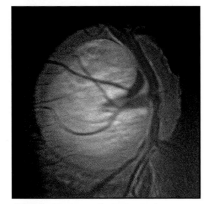

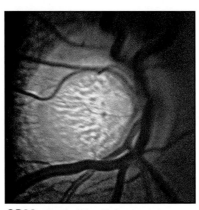

OP22. Concentric Enlargement of Optic Disc
Some inferior and temporal neuroretinal thinning.
© 2003 Dr. Yan

OP23. Optic Disc Enlargement
Slight thinning of neuroretinal rim inferiorly and temporally, deepening of cup, **development of pallor** (late finding of glaucoma).

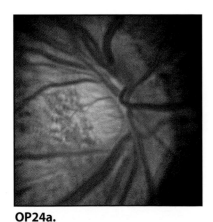

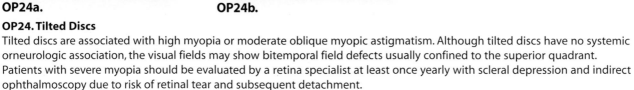

OP24a.

OP24b.

OP24. Tilted Discs
Tilted discs are associated with high myopia or moderate oblique myopic astigmatism. Although tilted discs have no systemic orneurologic association, the visual fields may show bitemporal field defects usually confined to the superior quadrant.
Patients with severe myopia should be evaluated by a retina specialist at least once yearly with scleral depression and indirect ophthalmoscopy due to risk of retinal tear and subsequent detachment.

Fundoscopy

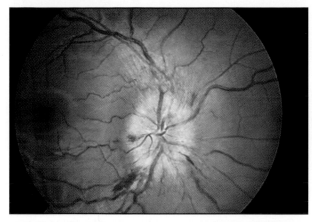

OP25. Papilledema
Elevated congested disc with indistinct margins, flame-shaped hemorrhages, and dilated tortuous vessels.

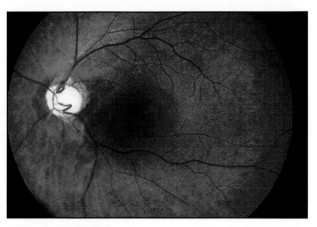

OP26. Optic Atrophy
Pallor of optic disc with sharp margins; attenuated vessels.

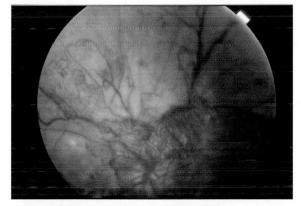

OP27. Proliferative Diabetic Retinopathy
Fan-shaped network of new blood vessels branching onto optic disc (neovascularization). Also note dot hemorrhages and microaneurysms.

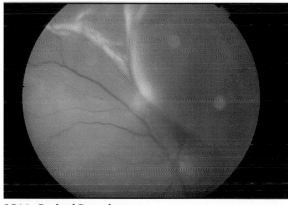

OP28. Retinal Detachment
Bullous retinal detachment with retinal folds on temporal aspect.

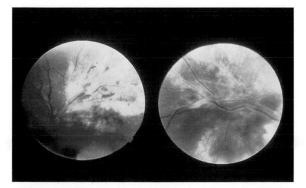

OP29. Cytomegalovirus Retinitis
White exudate surrounding hemorrhages and areas of necrosis. Distinct border between diseased and normal retina.

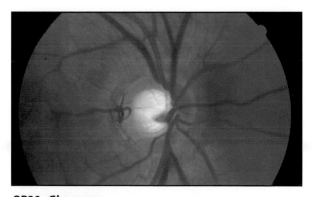

OP30. Glaucoma
Asymmetrical increase of cup:disc ratio (0.8). Cupping seen where vessels disappear over the edge of the attenuated rim.

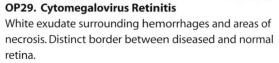

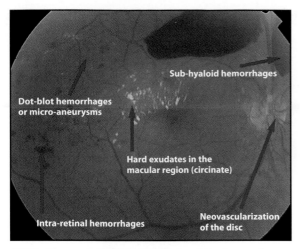

OP31. Photograph of the right eye with advanced proliferative diabetic retinopathy.

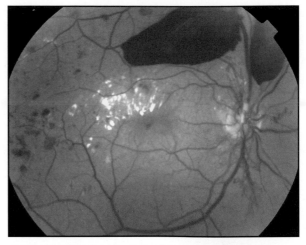

OP32. Red-free image of the right fundus of a patient with proliferative diabetic retinopathy as was illustrated previously in the color picture.

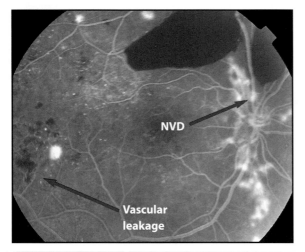

OP33. Early fluorescein angiography picture of the above eye showing areas of vascular leakage near the disc (NVD) and elsewhere (intra-retinal haemorrhages).

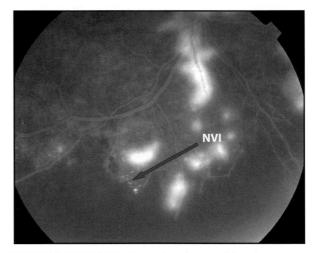

OP34. Fluorescein angiography picture of the above eye showing areas of vascular leakage elsewhere (NVE)

Otolaryngology

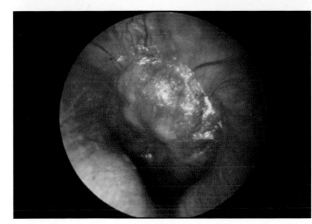

OT1. Acute Otitis Media (AOM)
Bulging, hyperemic tympanic membrane with indistinct landmarks.

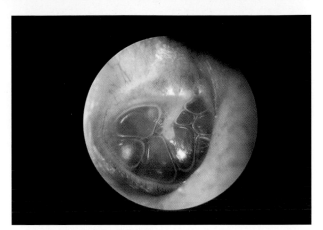

OT2. Serous Otitis Media
Air bubbles and serous fluid behind retracted amber tympanic membrane.
(Courtesy Dr. M. Hawke)

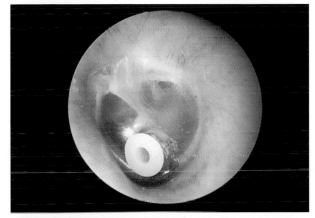

OT3. Tympanostomy Tube
Plastic tube placed in inferior portion of tympanic membrane.
(Courtesy Dr. M. Hawke)

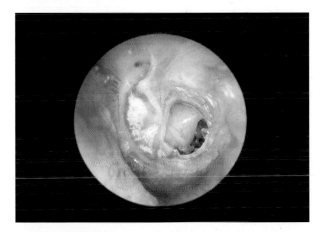

OT4. Perforated Tympanic Membrane
(Courtesy Dr. M. Hawke)

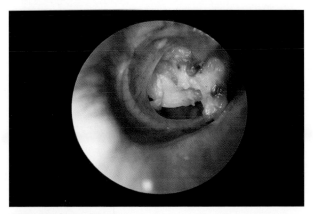

OT5. Cholesteatoma
Cyst-like mass lined with keratinized squamous epithelium and filled with desquamating debris in the middle ear. Progressive enlargement may lead to bony/soft tissue destruction.
(Courtesy Dr. M. Hawke)

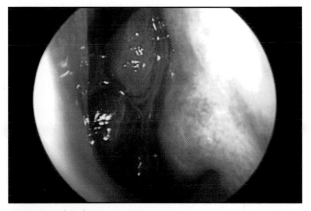

OT6. Nasal Polyps
Grape-like swellings hanging down from the sinuses into the nose. They are thought to result from an inflammatory response within the sinus mucosa.
(Courtesy Dr. M. Carr)

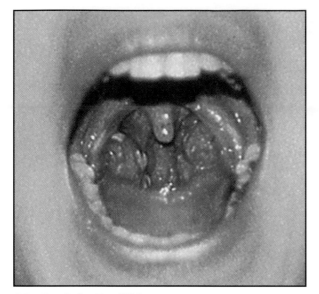

OT7. Exudative Tonsillitis
Enlarged and inflamed tonsils with purulent exudate in a patient with mononucleosis.
(Courtesy Dr. A. Waitzman)

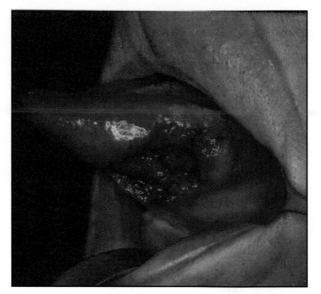

OT8. Carcinoma of Tongue
These are almost always squamous cell carcinomas (SCC) and occur as a result of exposure to tobacco, alcohol, and betel nut root.
(Courtesy Dr. D. Brown)

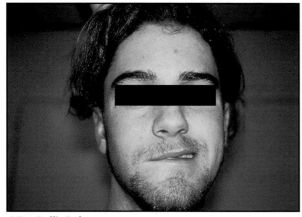

OT9. Bell's Palsy
Unilateral right facial nerve paralysis. Note patient smiling with mouth droop and loss of nasolabial fold.
(Courtesy Dr. A. Waitzman)

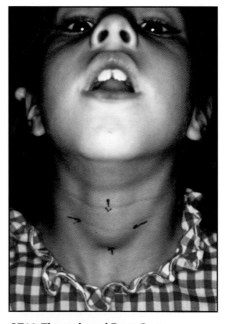

OT10. Thyroglossal Duct Cyst
Firm midline mass that moves up and down with swallowing.

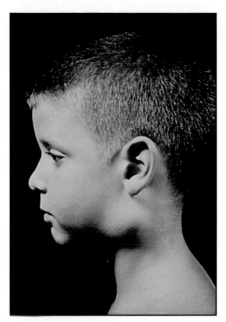

OT11. Branchial Cleft Cyst
Persistence of branchial cleft remnant as firm cystic mass in lateral neck.

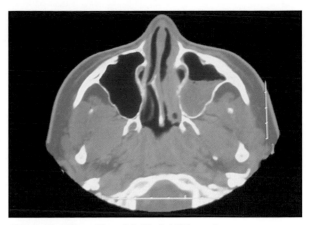

OT12. Maxillary Sinusitis (Axial CT scan)
Air-fluid level in left maxillary sinus.
(Courtesy Dr. A. Waitzman)

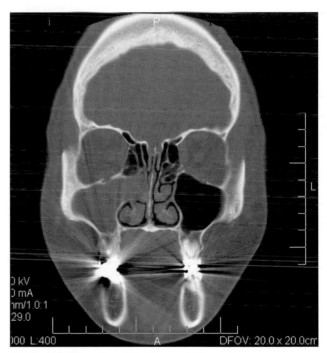

OT13. Maxillary Sinusitis (Coronal CT scan)
Right sided maxillary sinusitis.
(Courtesy Dr. M. Carr)

Pediatrics

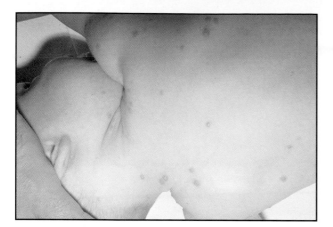

P1. Chicken Pox
Maculopapular rash on trunk progressing to vesicles and to crusts.
(Courtesy Dr. M. Mian)

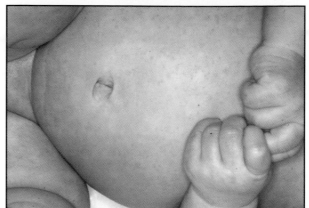

P2. Roseola
Diffuse maculopapular rash.
(Courtesy The Hospital for Sick Children Slide Library, Toronto)

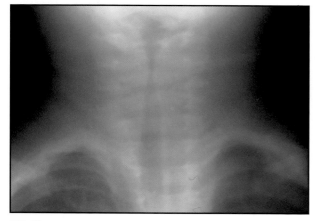

P3. Croup
"Steeple sign" showing inflammation of tissues in narrow subglottic space.
(Courtesy Dr. M. Mian)

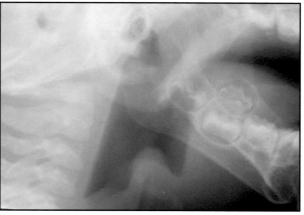

P4. Epiglottitis
"Thumb sign" showing a swollen epiglottis seen just at level of hyoid bone.
(Courtesy Dr. M. Mian)

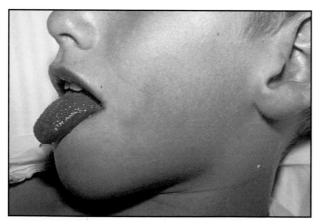

P5. Scarlet Fever
Strawberry tongue.
(Courtesy Dr. M. Mian)

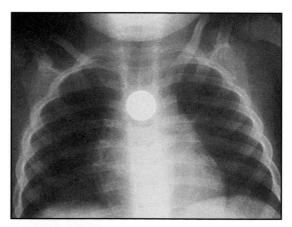

P6. Foreign Body
Coin lodged in esophagus.
(Courtesy Dr. A. Waitzman)

Plastic Surgery

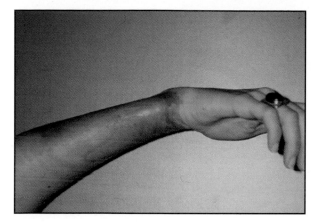

**PL1. 1st degree burn
(superficial partial thickness)**
Superficial partial thickness burn to forearm.
Note the presence of unroofed blisters.

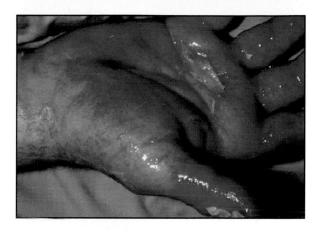

**PL2. 2nd degree burn
(deep partial thickness)**
Deep partial thickness burn to palm. The wound has a wet,
variable appearance, with both pale and red areas.

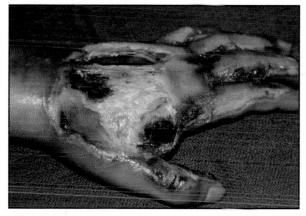

**PL3. 3rd degree burn
(full thickness)**
Full thickness burn to dorsum of hand. Thrombosed vessels and
underlying adipose tissue are clearly visible.

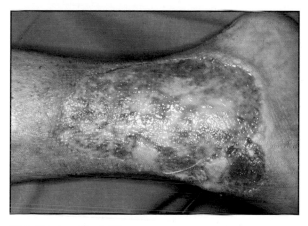

PL4. Venous Stasis Ulcer
(Courtesy Dr. A. Freiberg)

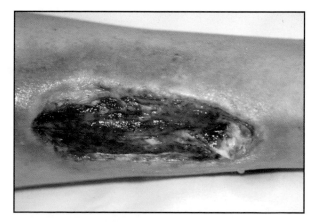

PL5. Arterial Ischemic Ulcer
(Courtesy Dr. A. Freiberg)

Rheumatology

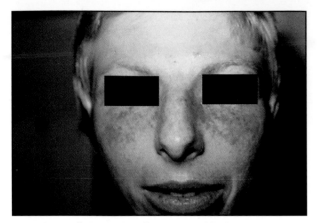

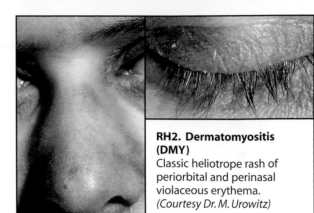

RH2. Dermatomyositis (DMY)
Classic heliotrope rash of periorbital and perinasal violaceous erythema.
(Courtesy Dr. M. Urowitz)

RH1. Systemic Lupus Erythematosus (SLE)
Prominent scaly fixed erythema, flat or raised over malar eminences, tending to spare nasolabial folds ("butterfly rash").

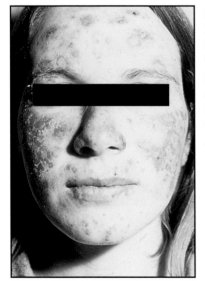

**RH3.
Discoid Lupus Erythematosus**
Violaceous, hyperpigmented, atrophic plaques; keratotic scale with follicular plugging and scarring.
(Courtesy Dr. L. From)

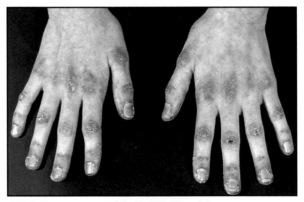

RH4. Dermatomyositis (DMY) (Hands)
Erythematous flat-topped scaling papules over the knuckles showing Gottron's papules and periungal telangiectasia.
(Courtesy The Hospital for Sick Children Slide Library, Toronto)

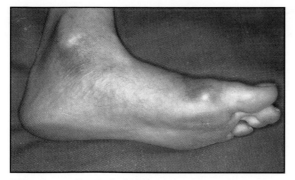

RH5. Acute Gouty Arthritis
Classic inflammation resembling cellulitis of the first metatarsophalangeal (MTP) joint, referred to as podagra. The first MTP is the most common site of initial involvement.
(Courtesy Dr. A. Fam)

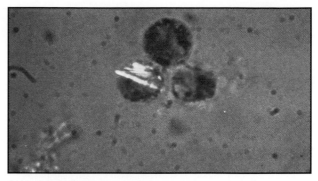

RH6. Acute Gout
Monosodium Urate Crystals
Polarized light microscopy showing monosodium urate crystals. Note the negative birefringence (yellow) of needle-shaped crystals versus the rhomboid-shaped and positively birefringent (blue) crystals of crystal pyrophosphate disease (CPPD).
(Courtesy Dr. A. Fam)

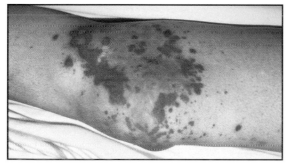

RH7. Vasculitis
Note purpuric papules.
(Courtesy Dr. A. Fam)

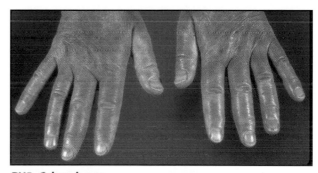

RH8. Scleroderma
Sclerodactyly showing bilateral swelling, a shiny wax-like appearance, and tapering of the fingers. May also note digital ulcers, nailfold telangiectasia, and periarticular calcinosis. Flexion contractures present in advanced disease.
(Courtesy Dr. A. Fam)

Urology

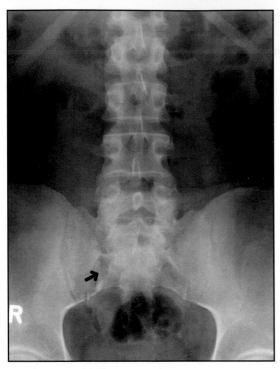

U1. Ureteric Calculus
Small stone seen at right pelvic brim.

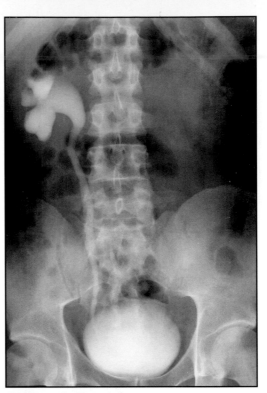

U2. Ureteric Obstruction
Intravenous pyelogram (IVP) (1 hour post-dye injection) showing right hydronephrosis, hydroureter, dilated renal pelvis and calyx.

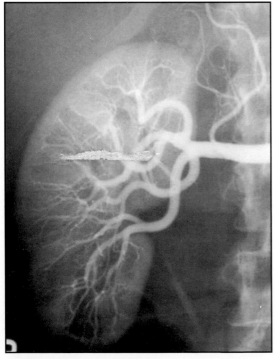

U3. Normal Renal Arteriogram

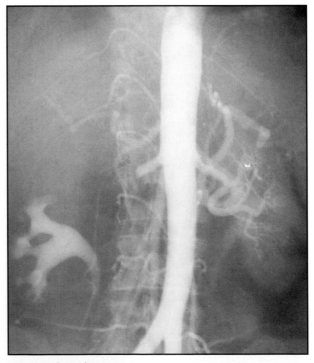

U4. Renal Angiogram